"In this remarkable book, Mark Freeman makes a powerful case for reimagining psychology as an integral practice of the humanities. This is an elegant, passionate, and persuasive plea for a deeply humane approach to our understanding of the psyche – one more poetically and ethically attuned to what it means to be human. It is timely and bold."

Richard Kearney, *Charles B. Seelig Chair of Philosophy, Boston College, USA*

"At a time when despair rises Mark Freeman – a stunning writer, theorist and humanistic psychologist – offers a resurrection story for Psychology, inviting us to move forward toward uncertainty, curiosity, the poetic and the unknown. The world needs us to take up his challenge. Thanks, Mark, for pouring your heart, desire and radical love into a field that so needs to be watered by your light. Readers – Put down your power points, buy this book and teach it! In elite universities and even more so in community colleges where young people have desires, stories to tell, anxieties to express, wounds to heal and radical visions to narrate, if only we asked."

Michelle Fine, *Distinguished Professor of Critical Psychology, The Graduate Center, CUNY and Visiting Professor at University of South Africa*

"The discipline of psychology has reached a negative-dialectical stage where another randomly chosen empirical study may contribute to normal science, and can be added to the millions of published articles, but fails to advance substantive knowledge about the mental being of persons. In contrast, Mark Freeman's book invigorates theoretical streams of thinking and provides proof of the psychological humanities' relevance and potential for an integrative understanding of the human condition. His ideas outline a humble framework for a new psychology that is onto-epistemically satisfying, ethical, as well as revolutionary."

Thomas Teo, *Professor of Psychology, York University, Canada*

"In this work, Freeman sketches the contours of a psychological humanities, an alternative approach to psychological inquiry which remains faithful to 'mystery' and 'messiness' of human life. Freeman beautifully illustrates its potential with rich examples, the most potent of which come from his own life. If the goal is to understand humanity in all its rich texture and complexity, Freeman's 'poetic science' speaks directly and compellingly to that goal. I believe this is an essential book for all students and researchers of psychology."

Kathleen L. Slaney, *Professor of Psychology, Simon Fraser University, Canada*

Toward the Psychological Humanities

Mark Freeman's inspiring account of the burgeoning field of the psychological humanities presents a clear and compelling vision of what the discipline of psychology might become.

Valuable though the scientific perspective has been for advancing the discipline, Freeman maintains that significant dimensions of the human experience elude this perspective and call for an entirely different kind of psychology, one more closely tied to the arts and humanities. Issuing his call for the psychological humanities in the form of a ten-chapter "manifesto," Freeman's groundbreaking book offers a comprehensive rationale for a more inclusive, pluralistic, and artful approach to exploring the psychological world in all of its potential complexity, obscurity, and beauty.

Engaging and accessible, this bold, provocative book is destined to spark significant discussion and debate in audiences including advanced undergraduates, postgraduates, and professionals in the field of psychology with interests in theoretical and philosophical psychology, history of psychology, clinical psychology, humanistic psychology, and qualitative psychology. It will also be welcomed by those in philosophy, literature, and the arts, as well as anyone intrigued by psychological life who may be interested in encountering a vital new approach to examining the human condition.

Mark Freeman is Distinguished Professor of Ethics and Society in the Department of Psychology at the College of the Holy Cross, USA. His writings include *Rewriting the Self: History, Memory, Narrative*; *Hindsight: The Promise and Peril of Looking Backward*; *The Priority of the Other: Thinking and Living Beyond the Self*; and *Do I Look at You With Love? Reimagining the Story of Dementia.*

Advances in Theoretical and Philosophical Psychology
Brent D. Slife, Series Editor

Critical Psychology Praxis: Psychosocial Non-Alignment to Modernity/ Coloniality
Robert K. Beshara

Hermeneutic Dialogue and Shaping the Landscape of Theoretical and Philosophical Psychology: The Work of Frank Richardson
Robert C. Bishop

Global Pandemics and Epistemic Crises in Psychology: A Socio-Philosophical Approach
Martin Dege and Irene Strasser

Hermeneutic Approaches to Interpretive Research: Dissertations In a Different Key
Philip Cushman

A Humane Vision of Clinical Psychology, Volume 1: The Theoretical Basis for a Compassionate Psychotherapy
Robert A. Graceffo

A Humane Vision of Clinical Psychology, Volume 2: Explorations into the Practice of Compassionate Psychotherapy
Robert A. Graceffo

A Philosophical Perspective on Folk Moral Objectivism
Thomas Pölzler

A Psychological Perspective on Folk Moral Objectivism
Jennifer Cole Wright

Toward the Psychological Humanities: A Modest Manifesto for the Future of Psychology
Mark Freeman

For more information about this series, please visit www.routledge.com/Advances-in-Theoretical-and-Philosophical-Psychology/book-series/TPP

Toward the Psychological Humanities

A Modest Manifesto for the Future of Psychology

Mark Freeman

Routledge
Taylor & Francis Group
LONDON AND NEW YORK

First published 2024
by Routledge
4 Park Square, Milton Park, Abingdon, Oxon OX14 4RN

and by Routledge
605 Third Avenue, New York, NY 10158

Routledge is an imprint of the Taylor & Francis Group, an informa business

British Library Cataloguing-in-Publication Data
A catalogue record for this book is available from the British Library

Library of Congress Cataloging-in-Publication Data
Names: Freeman, Mark Philip, 1955– author.
Title: Toward the psychological humanities : a modest manifesto for the future of psychology / Mark Freeman.
Description: New York, NY : Routledge, 2024. | Series: Advances in theoretical and philosophical psychology | Includes bibliographical references and index. | Summary: "Mark Freeman's inspiring account of the burgeoning field of the psychological humanities presents a clear and compelling vision of what the discipline of psychology might become. Engaging and accessible, this bold, provocative book is destined to spark significant discussion and debate in audiences including advanced undergraduates, postgraduates, and professionals in the field of psychology with interests in theoretical and philosophical psychology"—Provided by publisher.
Identifiers: LCCN 2023015768 (print) | LCCN 2023015769 (ebook) | ISBN 9781032563305 (paperback) | ISBN 9780367340490 (hardback) | ISBN 9780429323652 (ebook)
Subjects: LCSH: Psychology—Philosophy. | Humanities—Psychological aspects.
Classification: LCC BF38 .F726 2024 (print) | LCC BF38 (ebook) | DDC 150.1—dc23/eng/20230504
LC record available at https://lccn.loc.gov/2023015768
LC ebook record available at https://lccn.loc.gov/2023015769

ISBN: 978-0-367-34049-0 (hbk)
ISBN: 978-1-032-56330-5 (pbk)
ISBN: 978-0-429-32365-2 (ebk)

DOI: 10.4324/9780429323652

Contents

Acknowledgments

So many people inspired this work, from my grad school days at the University of Chicago all the way to my colleagues and friends at Holy Cross, where I have been teaching since 1986. For this particular book and series, though, I want to acknowledge my colleagues and friends from Division 24 (the Society for Theoretical and Philosophical Psychology), Division 32 (the Society for Humanistic Psychology), and the Society for Qualitative Inquiry in Psychology (a section of Division 5, Quantitative and Qualitative Methods), especially: Michael Bamberg, Sunil Bhatia, Robert Bishop, Scott Churchill, Michelle Fine, Roger Frie, Ken Gergen, David Goodman, Nisha Gupta, Ruthellen Josselson, Suzanne Kirschner, Jack Martin, Mary Beth Morrissey, Frank Richardson, Louis Sass, Kate Slaney, Brent Slife, Jeff Sugarman, and Thomas Teo.

I also want to acknowledge and express some special gratitude to Phil Cushman, someone tragically taken from us too soon, whose generous spirit remains very much alive, in the pages of this book, in the work many of us do, and in the lives we lead.

Finally, I want to acknowledge my family, especially my wife Debbie, who has been with me every step of the way for this book and everything else I've done through the years. I know this hasn't always been easy to do. For one, doing this kind of work takes a lot of time and attention. For another, I can sometimes get wrapped up in my own thinking and writing, and can be difficult to deal with at these times (among others). It's been my great good fortune to have someone beside me through it all.

Thank you, all.

This book represents a synthesis of much of the work I have done over the course of nearly 40 years. Although none of the chapters found here reproduce in full work that has been published elsewhere, a number of them do in fact make significant contact with this earlier work. Articles and chapters drawn upon significantly include "Theory beyond theory" (2000, *Theory & Psychology*, *10*, 71–77), "Wissenschaft und Narration" (2007, *Journal für*

Psychologie, 15, 1–29), "Psychoanalysis, narrative psychology, and the meaning of 'science'" (2007, *Psychoanalytic Inquiry, 27*, 583–601), "Qualitative inquiry and the self-realization of psychological science" (2014, *Qualitative Inquiry, 20*, 119–126), "Toward a poetics of the Other: New directions in post-scientific psychology" (2019, in T. Teo (Ed.), *Re-envisioning Theoretical Psychology: Diverging Ideas and Practices*, pp. 1–24 [Palgrave Macmillan]), "Heeding the face of the Other: A case study in relational ethics" (2019, *Human Arenas, 2*, 416–432), "Psychology as literature: Narrative knowing and the project of the psychological humanities" (2020, in J. Sugarman & J. Martin (Eds.), *A Humanities Approach to the Psychology of Personhood*, pp. 30–48 [Routledge]), "The mystery of identity: Fundamental questions, elusive answers" (2021, in M. Bamberg, C. Demuth, & M. Watzlawik (Eds.), *The Cambridge Handbook of Identity*, pp. 77–97 [Cambridge University Press]), and "How does the world become ecstatic? Notes on the hermeneutics of transcendence" (2021, in R. Bishop (Ed.), *Hermeneutic Dialogue and Shaping the Landscape of Theoretical and Philosophical Psychology*, pp. 112–123 [Routledge]). I do select some choice words from other work too, but these articles and chapters are the ones I've drawn upon the most, and they have been instrumental in the evolution of the ideas pursued in this book. I am immensely grateful for having had the opportunity to get all this previous work into print and also to return to it, in the service of this larger project.

Series Foreword

Psychologists need to face the facts. Their commitment to empiricism for answering disciplinary questions does not prevent pivotal questions from arising that cannot be evaluated exclusively through empirical methods, hence the title of this series: *Advances in Theoretical and Philosophical Psychology*. For example, such moral questions as, "What is the nature of a good life?" are crucial to psychotherapists but are not answerable through empirical methods alone. And what of these methods? Many have worried that our current psychological means of investigation are not adequate for fully understanding the person (e.g., Gantt & Williams, 2018; Schiff, 2019). How do we address this concern through empirical methods without running headlong into the dilemma of methods investigating themselves? Such questions are in some sense philosophical, to be sure, but the discipline of psychology cannot advance even its own empirical agenda without addressing questions like these in defensible ways.

How then should the discipline of psychology deal with such distinctly theoretical and philosophical questions? We could leave the answers exclusively to professional philosophers, but this option would mean that the conceptual foundations of the discipline, including the conceptual framework of empiricism itself, are left to scholars who are *outside* the discipline. As undoubtedly helpful as philosophers are and will be, this situation would mean that the people doing the actual psychological work, psychologists themselves, are divorced from the people who formulate and re-formulate the conceptual foundations of that work. This division of labor would not seem to serve the long-term viability of the discipline.

Instead, the founders of psychology—scholars such as Wundt, Freud, and James—recognized the importance of psychologists in formulating their own foundations. These parents of psychology not only did their own theorizing, in cooperation with many other disciplines; they also realized the significance of psychologists continuously *re*-examining these theories and philosophies. This re-examination process allowed for the people most directly involved in and knowledgeable about the discipline to be the ones to decide *what* changes were needed, and *how* such changes would best be implemented. This book series is dedicated to that task, the examining and re-examining of psychology's foundations.

Brent D. Slife, Series Editor

References

Gantt, E., & Williams, R. (2018). *On hijacking science: Exploring the nature and consequences of overreach in psychology*. London: Routledge.

Schiff, B. (2019). *Situating qualitative methods in psychological science*. London: Routledge.

Introduction

Time for a Change

Audacious though it may sound (and be), my primary aim in proposing this book is to offer my own integrated vision of what the discipline of psychology might become. I had the opportunity to do so, in briefer form, at the 2015 meeting of the American Psychological Association, when I presented my Presidential Address to my colleagues in Division 24 of the APA (the Society for Theoretical and Philosophical Psychology). That presentation carried the title "What Should Psychology Become? A Modest Manifesto." As for the substance of this manifesto, I offered it in the form of ten principles—or what I have come to think of as "meditations"—which, taken together, might serve to articulate the broad vision being advanced. I return to these same principles, with some significant modifications, in the pages to follow, in the form of ten brief chapters, each of which is dedicated to the principle in question. I will say more about this strategy shortly.

Given the fact that I am addressing multiple principles in the proposed book, it is difficult to offer a concise thesis-like argument. Nevertheless, in response to the broad question of what psychology might become, I can say the following, in mouthful, tenfold form: I suggest that psychology ought to become a gentler discipline, one that is more open to the mystery of being human; interpretively humble; reverential toward reality, in all of its fullness; attuned to the poetic dimension both of human lives and psychological inquiry; oriented toward thinking "Otherwise" about the human condition; faithful to the messiness and beauty of other persons; willing to chart the otherness within, that is, the elusive phenomenon that goes by the name of the "self"; able to respect and engage with the ineffable, especially as manifested in ostensibly transcendent experience; committed to serving humanity; and, last but not least, ready to tear down the walls that have hemmed psychology in, and to do so in the name not of violence but love. Throughout all of these urgings, I also suggest that psychology ought to be more artful in carrying out its work—not for the sake of ornamentation or flourish but for the sake of doing justice and practicing fidelity to reality. This makes for a much more unwieldy psychology, requiring quite different methods, methodologies, and, perhaps most fundamentally, *mindsets*, ones that are closer to the arts and

DOI: 10.4324/9780429323652-1

humanities than to the sciences, at least as customarily conceived and defined. I have come to frame such a psychology as a *poetics of the Other* (Freeman, 2019a, 2020, 2022a), and I see it as a part of what has come to be known as the "psychological humanities" (Sugarman & Martin, 2020a; Teo, 2017). With this broad vision in hand, I offer the hope that we might craft a psychology that is substantially better—more adequate, more humane, more ethically sound, and more *true*—than the one we have now.

When I was in the process of drafting the talk that gave rise to this book, the Hoffman Report, which detailed some notable APA members' contributions to "enhanced interrogation" techniques (i.e., torture) had recently come out. I therefore needed to change some of what I had planned to say. At the same time, I found myself reluctant to have the Report dominate my—or the Division's—thinking. This isn't because I saw it as insignificant; it was, and remains, very significant. It's not because I wanted to avoid it either. It's because I had yet to find it a particularly valuable site for *thinking*—which, through it all, I consider the main charge of the Division. Is any of what happened a radical surprise? Did we learn anything new about the corruptibility of people or the nature of bureaucracies or the diffusion of responsibility or the separation of the empirical and the ethical? I'm not sure. What we had, and still have, is a stain, a very ugly stain, which for many of us called into question why we were even a part of this organization.

As I mentioned in one of my notes to the Division shortly after the release of the Hoffman report, this was hardly the first time our allegiance to the APA had been called into question. Speaking for myself, I have been calling it into question for years, and for a whole slew of reasons. For one, as some of my colleagues in the Psychology Department at Holy Cross have reminded me, for about 35 years now, it's not even clear that I am a psychologist. For another, I continue to think that it's a really weird—and, at times, positively wrongheaded and deplorable—discipline. I don't really know why my response to the discipline has been as visceral as it is, but it's been this way ever since I was an undergraduate, when I learned that the discipline had very little to do with actual people. There is no question but that I, like many others, had an overly romantic and naive view of what psychology was all about. But I was still taken aback by its sheer . . . inhumanity? Scientism? False consciousness? Fetishistic fascination with method? (I'm skimming the surface.) Then there was this mammoth organization that, for some reason or other, many of us agreed to join. It took me a while to do so, and then, when I did join, I was very occasional—so much so that, one time when I showed up after a few years of absence, my friend the late Phil Cushman said something like, "Well, look who's here" or "Nice of you to join us" or something like that. "Hmmm," I said to myself. Am I supposed to really be a part of this thing? I hadn't wanted to appear standoffish, but the fact is, I found the organization and institutional end of things to be pretty alienating. All the knickknacks being hawked at the book display. The new technologies. The little rubber brains that were handed out. It wasn't a particularly cool crowd either. Given the nature of the discipline, that's not surprising.

Anyway, somehow or other, I became a regular. It wasn't because of the opportunity to give 12–15-minute papers at a 15,000-person conference in some faraway city filled with psychologists, the vast majority of whose work I had (and have) absolutely no interest in (nor they in mine). It wasn't because of all of those little trinkets and snacks you can get at the book display either (though I do have some). And it wasn't because of all the wonderful networking opportunities available. I'm not really a networker type.

It was around the time of drafting some of these words that things started getting a little scary. Why *was* I there? Why were *any* of us there? Although some of what I'm saying probably sounds unduly negative and snarky to some readers, I'm guessing that quite a few can identify with it too. At different times in its history, the Division might well have been called the "Society for Those Deeply Disaffected with Mainstream Psychology Desperately in Search of a New Way." But this is curious too. Why should we spend so much time critiquing a discipline and an organization that many of us found seriously wanting? And why were we so dedicated to creating funky new theories and metatheories (etc.) that would more than likely not make their way much further than the gates of the Division?

One reason I have remained with the Division—and I'm guessing this is true for many—is that it's been the home of some incredible people, quite a few of whom have become not just good colleagues but real friends, wonderful friends, people with whom to break bread, share drinks and jokes and all the while share ideas too, and questions, of the sort that nag at us and make us want to think and write about things we care about. To have a space where all this is possible is no small thing, and I am extremely grateful for it.

Having offered this somewhat gushy qualification, let me qualify *it* by saying that none of this bread-breaking and drinking and thinking and so on has to happen under the rather massive tent of the APA. And indeed some of it doesn't. Should *any* of it? "Stay the course," I said in one of my post-Hoffman report notes to the Division, and let's "see whether we might be able to work together to build a better, more ethically sound organization." That still sounds right to me, but not loudly so. In fact, if truth be told, I care less about the organization than I do about the discipline of psychology itself—which, for me as for many others, remains, well, kind of weird.

This leads me to another qualification of sorts, and it's one that often surprises my students. Why, they sometimes ask, didn't you go into philosophy or literature or one of the arts? The reason, I say, is that psychology—at its best—is a noble and wonderful endeavor. Exploring the human condition, in all of its complexity and messiness and possible beauty? Trying to fathom who we are, and why, and doing so through looking at the lives of real flesh and blood people, including ourselves? Even if it's not a cool discipline, it's done a lot of cool stuff and has the potential to do lots more. I even go so far as to say that, if I had to do it all over again, I'd still be a psychologist (which may even be true). Actually, though, it would be more appropriate to say: I would be a person who thinks and writes about psychological issues in a way that I find adequate to the messiness and possible beauty of the human experience. Why the qualification? Well, I might say, psychology—at its best—is often carried out by people who aren't psychologists. They're writers, painters, or musicians, people who are so fascinated and intrigued by *life* that they devote their lives to exploring it. Curiously enough, those who call themselves psychologists are much less likely to do so. What a strange, and ironic, situation! It's a tragic one too, especially for those who might have imagined that they too would have the opportunity for such imaginative exploration, only to learn that that's not what psychology tends to do.

Like many others in theoretical and philosophical psychology, I have spent a good portion of my career developing critiques of the discipline. I have no regrets about doing so; the critical moment is an important one. But as I argued a while back at one of the midwinter meetings of the Division, it was imperative to supplement critique with *creation*. That is, it was, it is, imperative to develop a vision of how the discipline might change in order to more fully realize itself. Since this seems to be the qualification section, let me offer one more. The vision I am about to offer is, inevitably and irrevocably, *mine*. I say this not for the sake of touting my own originality; plenty of people have been part of this vision and would no doubt sign on to much of it. Rather, I say it because it embodies a quite contestable image of what the discipline ought to be—one that flies in the face of many of its most thoroughgoing and long-standing commitments. I also say it because it is but one version, or one dimension, of what the psychological humanities might be.

Enough of these qualifications. It's time to get on with it. Here is a brief outline of the ten chapters to follow, each of which embodies (what I take to be) one of the fundamental "urges" integral to the vision at hand.

Chapter 1, "Openness to the Mystery," has as its fundamental premise the fact that we really don't know who and what we are. This hasn't stopped psychologists, philosophers, and others from proclaiming that they do in fact know: We are nothing but a constellation of behaviors. We are nothing but a complex, no doubt egocentric, organism. We are nothing but a soulless product of brain processes. (And so forth and so on.) These assertions may be taken as axiomatic and unassailable. But there is arrogance and hubris at work in such proclamations, and in the face of them, it is important for psychology to remain open to the mystery of the human being and to avow, humbly, that much of psychological inquiry begins, or ought to begin, in unknowing and wonder.

Chapter 2, "Interpretive Humility," is about the fact that, when it comes to understanding, or trying to understand, human experience on a deeper plane—for instance, trying to account for how and why we have become who we are—there is no getting around the process of interpretation and no getting around the fact that, try as we might to finalize such interpretation and "seal the deal" of understanding, it is patently impossible to do so. There is no need to see this as some sort of failure, however. Instead, it is profound testimony to the notion that, not unlike works of literature and artworks, human reality is itself an "open work," requiring us to attend interpretively to its complexity, multivocality, and uncontainability.

Chapter 3, "Reverence for the Real," draws significantly on an important essay by Heidegger titled "Science and Reflection" and seeks to show how and why the idea of the "real," once conceived as an open, uncontainable region, became transformed into that which could be observed, cordoned off, and measured, culminating in a view of science that remains with us today, in psychology and elsewhere. Valuable thought this view of science may be, it has, arguably, led to the diminution of the very idea of reality, with the result that which falls outside its scope is variously set aside, ignored, or negated. In the face of this reductive diminution, it is imperative for psychology to be more reverential in its relationship to the real and more willing to embrace and engage with those features of the human experience that are most resistant to those objectifying schemes that seek to contain it.

Chapter 4, "Reaching for the Poetic," moves further in the direction Heidegger (1971), among others, would eventually move by suggesting that reverence for the real, in all of its uncontainable fullness and bounty, requires modes of attention and exploration that are poetic in nature, which, broadly conceived, means that they are oriented toward disclosing or "unconcealing" those features of reality, both human and nonhuman, that have gone unseen or under-seen, and are committed to doing so as faithfully as possible. This aim of reaching for the poetic may be seen by some as continuing to serve the interests of science—"poetic science" (Freeman, 2007a, 2011), as it might be called. However, it may also be seen as reaching beyond science, as customarily conceived, and leading instead to the psychological humanities.

Chapter 5, "Thinking Otherwise," posits that reaching for the poetic has as its corollary "thinking Otherwise" both about reality and about the discipline of psychology itself. This is because before psychology, and before the various ways in which we seek to understand, know, and speak, there is the *world*, both human and nonhuman, calling us out of ourselves and beyond ourselves. In framing things this way, we can plausibly speak of the *priority* of the Other (Freeman, 2014a), and in speaking of this priority, we can also begin to craft a *poetics* of the Other (Freeman, 2019a), firmly and well located within the psychological humanities.

Chapter 6, "Fidelity to the Other Persons," seeks to carry further the idea of a poetics of the Other in the context of encountering, understanding, and depicting the reality of other persons. The task is large, for both interpretive and ethical reasons. On the phenomenological and interpretive plane, one very basic challenge has to do with shedding the potentially calcified schemes we might bring to the task and truly engaging other persons in their otherness and difference. On the ethical plane, the challenge has to do with respecting the otherness of the other and doing justice to it in and through our own depictions. In this context, especially, doing so artfully is imperative, for only then will we truly practice the fidelity required.

Chapter 7, "Fidelity to the Otherness Within," explores the particularly daunting challenge of encountering, understanding, and depicting oneself through narrative. One notoriously difficult aspect of this challenge concerns the fact that, strictly speaking, there is no "object" there to behold but rather something that is, in essence, of our own making—a "me" coming before the eye of an "I," never to wholly be disentangled from it. Not surprisingly, this state of affairs has led some notable thinkers to conclude that the self is a fiction, as are any and all accounts we might possibly provide. Partially valid though this way of thinking about selfhood is, it is important to move beyond it. This means engaging with the otherness within, which, paradoxically, requires our ability to "unself" (Murdoch, 1970) ourselves sufficiently to behold, and depict, our own inevitably obscure reality.

Chapter 8, "A Space for the Ineffable," takes on the formidable, and for some controversial, challenge of including, within the scope of psychological inquiry, those ostensibly "transcendent" experiences, such as aesthetic and religious experiences, that, in their very ineffability, elude extant modes and that, consequently, have often been considered outside the scope of the discipline. Putting aside the question of whether such experiences truly bespeak a transcendent realm, understood as being outside the perimeter of the self and thus wholly, and truly, *other*, the task of exploring such experiences and doing justice to their sheer presence remains. This task is nothing less than that of seeking to engage and express the inexpressible, and if it cannot properly be done within the confines of the psychological sciences, it is only fitting that the psychological humanities rise to the occasion.

Chapter 9, "In the Service of Humanity (and Beyond)," begins by noting that some people may find some psychological humanities work wanting precisely by virtue of its ostensible uselessness. This stands to reason: Compared to an endeavor that seeks to explain, predict, control, and apply itself to important spheres of human and nonhuman functioning, some of the work that is situated under the umbrella of the psychological humanities, in their very lack of overt instrumentality, is likely to appear useless and gratuitous, perhaps a step backward from the great and undeniable progress the discipline has made. There may be an element of truth to aspects of this potential criticism. However, the manifest uselessness of the work being considered is in no way to be equated with its lack of *value*, for much of this work is in the service of humanity, understood in terms of both the entirety of the human species and, more important for present purposes, our attention to and care for one another. Such attention and care are not to be limited to the human world alone, however, but also to any and all features of the nonhuman world that demand them.

Chapter 10, “Tear Down the Walls (in the Name of Love),” sets forth the idea that the time has come for dismantling some central features of the contemporary discipline of psychology. Lest this seemingly destructive dimension be construed as insufficiently attuned to constructive and creative dimension of what’s needed, I consider these two moments to be of a piece, necessary and inevitable counterparts of a single, undivided process of reimagining the discipline. None of this seeks to undermine the good work that is currently being done or the people who carry it out. On the contrary, if some of us wish to tear down the walls, it must be done gently, in the name of love. Only this will place the psychological humanities on a sure and ethically sound footing, and only this will help lead to the kind of discipline many yearn for.

1 Openness to the Mystery

Here is a little secret that much of academic psychology has sought to keep under wraps: Much of psychological life is ambiguous, indefinite, and, ultimately, indeterminate. I have always loved how William James (1950 [1890]) speaks to this issue in his chapter on "The Stream of Thought" from *The Principles of Psychology*:

> The traditional psychology talks like one who should say a river consists of nothing but pailsful, spoonsful, quartpotsful, barrelsful, and other moulded forms of water. Even were the pails and the pots all actually standing in the stream, still between them the free water of consciousness would continue to flow. It is just this free water of consciousness that psychologists resolutely overlook.
>
> (p. 255)

To think that there were some who imagined that they could stop the flow with their various containers! What exactly is James calling for in this context? "It is, in short, the re-instatement of the vague to its proper place in our mental life which I am so anxious to press upon the attention" (p. 254). What a strange and wonderful mandate. The primacy of the vague! Let us recognize it and embrace it rather than drive it away through our various modes of methodological and theoretical entrapment.

James is mainly addressing the phenomenology of consciousness in his chapter, but the basic premise extends well beyond it. So often in psychology's history there have emerged movements to "stop the music," as it were, to imagine that by arriving at this principle of reinforcement or that neurotransmitter (or whatever), we will have arrived at the promised land of the unvarnished Truth about the human condition. We now know, it's often said: free will is an illusion; the self is an illusion; care for the other is a twisted guise for self-interest; there is no God. Psychologists often proclaim that they, we, *know* these things. *Finally*. It's not only audacious and arrogant. It's absurd.

DOI: 10.4324/9780429323652-2

Even very smart people fall prey to this problem. "We are all animal," Owen Flanagan (2003) announces, "and the brain is our soul" (p. xv). As Flanagan continues, in greater detail,

> Letting go of the belief in souls is a minimal requirement. In fact, desouling is the primary operation of the scientific image. "First surgery," we might call it. There are no such things as souls, or nonphysical minds. If such things did exist, . . . science would be unable to explain persons. But there aren't, so it can. Second, we will need to think of persons as parts of nature—as natural creatures completely obedient and responsive to natural law. The traditional religious view positions humans on the Great Chain of Being between animals on one side and angels and God on the other. This set of beliefs needs to be replaced. There are no angels, nor gods, and thus there is nothing—at least, no higher beings—for humans to be in-between. Humans don't possess some animal parts or instincts. We *are* animals. A complex and unusual animal, but at the end of the day, another animal.
>
> (p. 3)

Wow. Just Wow. I have no particular interest in disavowing my connection to animals or becoming a cheerleader for the soul, mind you (though there are worse things to be doing). No, my main goal in citing Flanagan in this context is to show the absurdly cocksure way in which some contemporary thinkers simply declare what they now *know*, or *think* they know, to be obvious, unassailable, and true. Do we *know* that there are no souls, or angels, or gods? Do we *know* that we are completely obedient and responsive to natural law? *Could* we know *any* of this?

Now, if all Flanagan was doing was saying, "For practical reasons having to do with psychology's aspiration of becoming a bona fide science, we need to set aside ideas like souls, angels, and gods and basically be agnostic about the matter," it would be harder to quibble (though I probably still would). But he is clearly doing something more, treating as axiomatic beliefs of his own that are every bit as open to question as the idols he seeks to smash. Lots of psychologists and philosophers do this sort of thing. "Grow up," they seem to be saying in one way or another. "Get with the program. It's the only valid one. How could you not accept this (you gullible, prescientific fool)?" Maybe they're right. Maybe there *are* no gods or nonphysical minds and all the rest. But the fact is, we don't know. Indeed, we don't know what the "proper" image of the human person is, and that's because there is no singular, unassailable way of framing who and what we are—or why we are even here. How could there be?

Now that I'm digging into the sheer audacity of these modern debunkers, I'll call attention to the fact that some of what they say is patently disingenuous too. Take the idea that free will is an illusion—which some of my students, having drunk the neuroscientific Kool-Aid, have somewhat uncritically bought into. Yes, of course; it's possible that everything we do, everything we are, is utterly and completely determined ahead of time. But there's actually ample evidence to the contrary from experience itself. Yes, of course; experience can lure us into believing things that aren't true. But it can also provide quite fleshy "data" that ought to be taken into account when proclaiming this or that about who and what we are. Then again, it's quite possible that some of the debunkers I've been referring to have already decided—ahead of time—that believing in phenomena like free will, mind, and self are simply outdated vestiges of primitive, or theological, thinking that have finally and fortunately been supplanted by the putatively uncontestable findings of Science. Don't get me wrong; I'm not against science! What I am calling into question here is the *a priori* assumption that it's the only true path to psychological knowledge and understanding and that our own intuitions, drawn from experience, are to be considered essentially untrustworthy.

Let me turn once more to William James, this time from *The Varieties of Religious Experience* (1982 [1902]), when he wonders whether "the claims of the sectarian scientist" are "premature":

> The experiences which we have been studying during this hour . . . plainly show the universe to be a more many-sided affair than any sect, even the scientific sect, allows for. What, in the end, are all our verifications but experiences that agree with more or less isolated systems of ideas (conceptual systems) that our minds have framed? But why in the name of common sense need we assume that only one such system of ideas can be true? The obvious outcome of our total experience is that the world can be handled according to many systems of ideas, and is so handled by different men, and will each time give some kind of characteristic profit, for which he cares, to the handler, while at the same time some other kind of profit has to be omitted or postponed. . . . Evidently, then, the science and the religion are both of them genuine keys for unlocking the world's treasure house to him who can use either of them practically. Just as evidently neither is exhaustive or exclusive of the other's simultaneous use. And why, after all, may not the world be so complex as to consist of many interpenetrating spheres of reality, which we can thus approach in alternation by using different conceptions and different attitudes?
>
> (pp. 122–123)

Why indeed?

C.G. Jung (1933) offers a related perspective when he writes:

> The spirit of the age cannot be compassed by the processes of human reason. It is an inclination, an emotional tendency that works upon weaker minds, through the unconscious, with an overwhelming force of suggestion that carries them along with it. To think otherwise than our contemporaries

> think is somehow illegitimate and disturbing; it is even indecent, morbid or blasphemous, and therefore socially dangerous for the individual. He is stupidly swimming against the social current. Just as formerly the assumption was unquestionable that everything that exists takes its rise from the creative will of a God who is spirit, so the nineteenth century discovered the equally unquestionable truth that everything arises from material causes. Today the psyche does not build itself a body, but on the contrary, matter, by chemical action, produces the psyche. This reversal of outlook would be ludicrous if it were not one of the outstanding features of the spirit of the age. It is the popular way of thinking, and therefore it is decent, reasonable, scientific and normal. Mind must be thought to be an epiphenomenon of matter. The same conclusion is reached if we say not "mind" but "psyche," and in place of matter speak of brain, hormones, instincts or drives. To grant the substantiality of the soul or psyche is repugnant to the spirit of the age, for to do so would heresy.
>
> (pp. 175–176)

In Jung's worldview, "there is a vast outer realm and an equally vast inner realm; between these two stands man, facing now one and now the other, and, according to his mood or disposition, taking the one for the absolute truth by denying or sacrificing the other" (p. 120). Here too, it's as if we cannot endure and abide the "vastness" of what we seek to know, and thus insistently reduce and absolutize. Modern psychology is especially guilty of doing so.

Alongside the dismantling of mind is the dismantling of self—or, if not dismantling, the "disillusioning" of self. The philosopher Mary Midgley (2014) tackles this issue head-on in her important book *Are You an Illusion?* "When something supposedly scientific clashes with common sense . . ., we naturally assume that common sense must be wrong." But the fact is, "common sense can grow and indeed it always is growing. It is not a fixed, unchanging formula that is always at odds with science." For Midgley, as for me,

> the way in which the universe works isn't confined to the things that the sciences tell us about it. That universe has hugely many aspects. It includes ourselves and our direct perceptions. It also includes the views of life that have been built up through aeons of human experience.

What we are considering here, she goes on to suggest, is less a "fixed formula" than "a great stretch of mental countryside full of different kinds of vegetation—life forms that keep developing to suit what is going on around them" (p. 3). So, when Francis Crick boldly proclaims that "You, your joys and sorrows, your memories and ambitions, your sense of personal identity and your free-will, are in fact no more than the behaviour of a vast assembly of nerve cells and their attendant molecules" (cited in Midgley, p. 5), she and I are inclined to conclude that Crick has indeed lost his mind and can no longer trust what his own experience tells him. Are joys and sorrows contingent on nerve cells and molecules? Probably—though even this is less of a "fact" than it is generally taken to be. Do these nerve cells and molecules help us understand and explain these deeply felt experiences? Hardly. Crick's statement is flat-out bizarre, and not because I just happen to believe otherwise but because it flies in the face of what common sense sometimes tells us. Are nerve cells and molecules more real than the experiences that may have brought about joys and sorrows? Only if we take "real" to be what exists in physical, material terms. And there is no compelling reason to do so whatsoever.

It is, of course, true that the self is not the kind of object that is found in the material world. Indeed, the self isn't an object at all and is, perhaps, better thought of as a kind of "presence" (Marcel, 1950). This is where some of the trouble begins. "As always in the higher reaches of thought," Marcel writes,

> we must be on our guard against the snares of language; when I distinguish the notion of a presence from that of an object, I run the risk, of course, of turning a presence for some of my listeners, into a sort of vaporized object that contrasts rather unfavourably with the tangible, solid, resistant objects that we are used to in what we call real life. But, in fact, when we say that a presence must not be thought of as an object, we mean that the very act by which we incline ourselves towards a presence is essentially different from that through which we grasp at any object; in the case of a presence, the very possibility of grasping at, of seizing, is excluded in principle.
> (p. 255)

Furthermore, "In so far as a presence, as such, lies beyond the grasp of any possible prehension, one might say that it also in some sense lies beyond the grasp of any possible *com*prehension" (p. 256). The self, as a kind of presence, can neither be prehended nor be comprehended, and so, compared to the world of objects, it (apparently) can't help but seem to some hopelessly vaporous, even illusory.

My aim in discussing this issue is not to elevate the self. It's high enough already, and I have no interest in raising it higher. My aim is instead to show that, in psychology's insistence on objectifying—which is to say, limiting its scope to what can be treated as object—it tends to occlude from view those very ungraspable presences that characterize much of psychological life. The problem, however, isn't only in the dismissal of the ungraspable, it's in the kind of attitude one takes to psychological life. Grasping an object is something *I* do; I hold it and manipulate it. A presence, on the other hand, "is something which can only be gathered to oneself or shut out from oneself, be welcomed or rebuffed" (Marcel, 1950, p. 255). It is *other*, and thus my attitude and my mode of comportment must be receptive, respectful, and humble. As Marcel goes on to note, "a philosophy of this sort is essentially of the nature of a kind of appeal to the listener or reader, of a kind of call upon his inner resources. In other words, such a philosophy could never be completely embodied into a kind of dogmatic exposition of which the listener or reader would merely have to grasp the content" (p. 262). It may therefore call for a quite different orientation than what is generally found in modern scientific psychology.

As Marilynne Robinson (2012) has succinctly written, "We live on a little island of the articulable, which we tend to mistake for reality itself" (p. 21). As a result, "[m]etaphysics has been abandoned as if it were a mistake sophisticated people could no longer make, an indulgence an illusionless world would no longer entertain" (2015, p. 190). As we have already seen, it's not just metaphysics that may be abandoned, but also, and more generally, those regions of human reality that elude the grasp of psychological science—at least as commonly understood.

"Assumptions and certitudes imposed on matters that should in fact be conceded to ignorance," Robinson continues, "warp and obstruct legitimate thought" (p. 192) by treating as knowable objects the realm of unknowable presences. For her,

> What we do not know should always function as a corrective to anything we think we do know. This depends, of course, on our diligently seeking our own ignorance. Science is the invaluable handmaiden of theology in that it tells us how astonishing and gigantically elusive are all the particulars of existence. And nothing is more unfathomable than ourselves, individually and collectively, at any given moment and from the earliest beginning of human time. . . . Thinking that we know more than we do, therefore rejecting what we are given as experience, blinds us to our ignorance, which is the deep darkness where truth abides.
>
> (p. 199)

I know this sort of language isn't for everybody. Robinson can sometimes sound ponderous and pompous. (I can too.) But what she has to say, here and elsewhere, is, in the end, a plea for both humility and wonder: before the vastness of the world and before the unfathomability of our very existence. None of this means that there aren't aspects of psychological life able to be fathomed and grasped. There are. But there is a very real sense, I think, in which, to paraphrase Robinson, much of psychology has mistaken this graspable "island" for the whole of reality.

But let us not gripe too much about psychology. Instead, as promised, let us move toward a more positive, forward-looking conception of the principle we have been exploring in this chapter. Openness to the mystery: What exactly does it mean? And why consider it a foundational principle in this modest attempt to reimagine psychology?

I am reminded here of the poet Wislawa Szymborska's Nobel Prize speech from 1996, "The Poet and the World," when she discusses the idea of inspiration. "Inspiration," she writes,

> is not the exclusive privilege of poets or artists. . . . There is, has been, and will always be a certain group of people whom inspiration visits. It's made up of all those who've consciously chosen their calling and do their job with love and imagination. It may include doctors, teachers, gardeners—and I could list a hundred more professions. Their work becomes one continuous adventure as long as they manage to keep discovering new challenges in it. Difficulties and setbacks never quell their curiosity. A swarm of new questions emerges from every problem they solve.

"Whatever inspiration is," Szymborska insists, "it's born from a continuous 'I don't know'."

> Poets, if they're genuine, must also keep repeating "I don't know." Each poem marks an effort to answer this statement, but as soon as the final period hits the page, the poet begins to hesitate, starts to realize that this particular answer was pure makeshift that's absolutely inadequate to boot. . . . The world—whatever we might think when terrified by its vastness and our own impotence, or embittered by its indifference to individual suffering, of people, animals, and perhaps even plants, for why are we so sure that plants feel no pain; whatever we might think of its expanses pierced by the rays of stars surrounded by planets we've just begun to discover, planets already dead? still dead? we just don't know; whatever we might think of this measureless theater to which we've got reserved tickets, but tickets whose lifespan is laughably short, bounded as it is by two arbitrary dates; whatever else we might think of this world—it is astonishing.

And so, Szymborska concludes, "It looks like poets will always have their work cut out for them." Psychologists too.

Who are we? "Oh, I know!" the psychologist often says. And the answers continue apace. But we don't know who we are, and at the foundational level being considered here, we can't. I say this not out of a sense of futility or disappointment but rather out of a sense of wonder. Can psychology keep wonder central to what it does? Can there be a discipline grounded in its own avowed commitment to holding open the nature of the human condition and embracing the mystery, such that "I don't know" becomes central to its rallying cry?

My answer is unlikely to surprise you: I don't know. There: the process has begun.

2 Interpretive Humility

Many years ago (1989), I wrote a brief story about one of my daughters, who suffered a mishap when she was a toddler. The piece is called "After a Fall," which the (*Parenting*) magazine editors insisted be followed by the words "Accidents happen—but what of your child's mishap occurred by your own hand?" Bound to get attention with those juicy words! It's really not what the piece is about, though. Here is how it opens:

> It's still too early to tell how much or in what way, but my two-year old daughter changed recently. Our whole family did, actually.
>
> One evening after dinner, Debbie, my wife, suggested that I take Brenna out on the porch to have dessert, which consisted of pieces of watermelon and peach. I sat with her on my lap, hoping she would try them. But after she'd picked at the fruit for a while, she insisted on getting down.
>
> A cloud now hangs over that dessert exchange, and everything that surrounds it is enshrouded in greenish darkness, like the kind before a storm. And though it's me who is supplying the tint here, through my awful memory, from now on it will be impossible to erase. Brenna got down and began to walk away, up the sidewalk, knowing that she wasn't supposed to do that alone. She took tiny steps, an inch at a time, peeking back at me, challenging. We've been through this many times. This time, I didn't bite: Rather than lunging after her, I sat calmly, making sure she didn't get out of my sight.
>
> But then she began to really move, and it was time to spring into action. As I advanced, plate of fruit still in my hand, her pace quickened further. I reached down with my free hand to pick her up. But she was still moving, and as I grabbed her around her belly—I don't know why I did it this way, since I know her center of gravity is higher—she pitched forward, onto the blacktop driveway next door.
>
> It really didn't seem like that terrible a fall, and despite her cries, I expected to turn her around and see some cuts and scratches. What I saw instead, with that damned plate in my hand even still, was blood, all over the bottom of her face and her new yellow t-shirt. Her bottom lip looked

DOI: 10.4324/9780429323652-3

> like it had been mauled by a vicious dog; it was in shreds, separated by deep gashes, and the two of us were suddenly bathed in enough horror to last a lifetime.
>
> (p. 112)

You get the idea.

To make a long story short, we had to cart Brenna off to the hospital to get her stitched up, she was pretty subdued on the ride home, and yes, it's true, "it was hard not to feel . . . that a part of our lives had ended, and hard to shake the dim but ceaseless recognition that if it hadn't been for me, everything would still be the same." Ugh. Fortunately, the next day, she basically seemed fine. "She even wanted to go outdoors to play," and "To top it off, before we knew it she'd left the porch and begun to steal up the street again, peeking backward, assuming we'd be in hot pursuit again, as always." A happy ending: "Brenna steals up the street, I run and whisk her off her feet—carefully—and we all go inside for lunch." But of course the ending can only be temporary,

> because the truth is that events retain a certain power, one that impels us to recall them again and again. Something happens, arising from a series of ordinary circumstances, and it gets carried along through your whole life. In fact, in some ways an accident of this sort isn't much different than meeting someone at a party, as I did, and marrying her later on, or studying with a professor who changes the direction of your dreams.
>
> (p. 112)

The whole series of events freaked me out, partly because I was partially responsible but also because I couldn't help but wonder how this early event would play itself out in her life. In what form would this horror last, and for how long? Would it be a lifetime? Would it persist, like the scar on her face, forever? Here was a trauma, or a would-be trauma, that might have affected her will, her playfulness, her sense of trust, and a slew of other things besides, and I desperately wanted to know how it would play itself out. But of course I couldn't. And the reason is that you can't know how a trauma is going to play itself out in the course of a life until that life has been lived. If even then . . .

The thing that probably freaked me out the most about the incident was my assumption, which was surely at least partially justified, that this trauma *would* get played out, in some form, in her life—which it probably has. How else could it be? I suppose it's possible, owing to her young age maybe, that the event just . . . disappeared, dispersed itself into thin air. More than likely, though, it entered into her psychical bloodstream in some way, not as a discrete "cause" that would produce some predictable "effect," but as a powerful formative experience that would somehow resonate throughout her life. So it is that I would sometimes find myself asking: What role has this event played in her life and her identity? How has it become inscribed? When she no longer wanted to play soccer, or when she wasn't first in line to volunteer for this or that special opportunity, I might have moaned pathetically to my wife, "It was that damn fall! It's sapped her of her sense of initiative!" Debbie, in turn, would tell me to get over it, that it had nothing to do with the stupid fall. She was probably right about this. But who knows? And how could we?

I don't have to go to Brenna's life to ask these sorts of questions. I can go to my own—the car accident I was in at 17, which left me in the intensive care unit, on the edge of death, for some days; losing a close friend to cancer the following year; losing my dad a few years later. (Interesting that examples of loss seem to come to mind first; I guess I need to look at that.) I could go positive too, citing our marriage, the birth of our children, the first article I ever published, and the first invitation to come to a big conference and give a keynote address. What do all these things *do*? How do they register in us?

Let me move more deeply into these questions by thinking further about the psychological consequences of my father's death, back in 1975, when I was 20 years old. An obvious question emerges: What impact did it have? Or, if we want to use somewhat gentler language: How did it move through me, form me? How did it contribute to the person I am today? Or, to use another kind of language altogether: How was it "metabolized"? How did it become filtered into my psychical bloodstream? That it was a formative event that has affected me profoundly seems unquestionable. But in what way? It's possible that his death affected me back then, but that its impact essentially passed, dispersed and dissipated. This strikes me as unlikely. The question, then, is whether there is a way to determine what its impact actually was. I tend to think not—certainly not in any discrete, fully discernible way. The problem is partly one of time scale. A month after his death, or a year, say, the situation would be different. The wound would still be wide open, and there would be fleshy memories of this or that experience or dimension of our relationship. So, it would hardly be a stretch to link the event of his death to its more immediate emotional and existential consequences. After a year, things would no doubt be substantially different. That death would now be a year old, and the very passing of that stretch of time would have yielded new emotional textures. And so it would be after five years, and ten, and 20, and on and on and on.

One could argue that the impact of my father's death can only be gauged as a function of the degree to which it entered my consciousness and whatever story I might wish to tell about the past. There are some versions of narrative knowing that might hold to this idea: The past is what we make it, it might be said, and the force of events can only be gleaned as a function of what one believes. Perhaps it is so: Perhaps we are nothing more than who we take, and make, ourselves to be. But this perspective doesn't quite work in my view, not least because there are surely features of our own self-formation about which we are largely unaware (Freeman, 2021a). More on this shortly.

One might also try to address these issues from the opposite direction, beginning from a present state and looking backward in order to determine how they may have come about. I had occasion to consider this very possibility during the course of a bicycle ride I took a while back, when I arrived at the realization that I had been living under a cloud for some time and began to muse about why that might be. What had been going on in my life that may have led me to this state? Then again, was this even the right question to ask? And here too, what was the proper time frame for launching my search? I had fallen into this sort of funk before, a number of times, actually. Times like these are reminiscent of the "black moods" my father would sometimes suffer from. Where did *his* come from, though? Were they genetic in some way? Had I gotten some of those genes? Then there was my mother; she herself had a reputation for being a "Pollyanna," but there had been some serious darkness on her side of the family too—a bipolar brother; a nephew, my cousin, who had put a gun to his head (and fired it); another cousin too, someone I spent a lot of time with as a kid and who I searched for once, on an island near Seattle, and couldn't find, only to learn not long after that she too had found the world too much to bear. Could this stuff be in there too? Was I the recipient of some weird genetic double-whammy? Perhaps. Oftentimes, moody phases like the one I just described seemed to arrive unbidden. They are often difficult to control too, difficult to move; I just need to wait them out, hope they pass quickly. Perhaps, therefore, they are just part of "who I am." Should I go with this interpretation? It's the easiest option in a way; I can spare myself the burden of searching further and just get on with it as best I can.

Then again, maybe this wasn't a matter of biology at all. I can remember the deep frustration and anger my father sometimes felt about aspects of his station in life—the job he had as a traveling salesman, the trunk of his car filled with samples, so tedious, all for the sake of making a decent living. (I have a memory of him looking into that trunk and visibly bemoaning his fate.) Boys often identify with their fathers. I had certainly taken on some of his traits, both good and not-so-good. Was this one? Had I somehow "learned" to deal with my own challenges and disappointments in life by unwittingly mimicking his rather dark way of dealing with them? He has been gone for more than 40 years now. Was grief involved, unfinished and unfinishable? Speaking of grief, I should also mention that my mother died about six years ago after a decade or so suffering from dementia. In her final years, she lived in a nursing home right in Worcester, where my family and I live. We saw her often; even when she was barely there, she remained a big part of our life. How did all of this figure in? It didn't make sense to consider her passing the "cause" of my malaise; again, I had gone through comparable phases in the past, before her dementia arrived. But it could certainly have been a contributing factor. In fact, it probably *had* to be. One doesn't just "get over" the death of a parent, especially not in circumstances like this one. Was I still in mourning?

It's possible, but it didn't feel like I was. What else might I look toward to try to get hold of what was going on? Where do I begin? And on what basis can I justify doing so? I could, and perhaps should, go back to the trials and tribulations of childhood. There is no question but that there were some complications back then, but I can't recall what they were with any clarity and, whatever they were, I don't think they were particularly exceptional. Much of my childhood, in fact, is downright foggy; add up all the minutes I can remember with any vividness at all—up until age 7, say—and there are precious few of them, virtually none of them sharp and clear. Do early experiences, or early phases of experience, "cause" things to emerge later on, in ways unbeknownst to us? Presumably, they do—fraught though the idea of "causation" is. But how can we possibly know how? *Can* we?

As far as I could tell, childhood was probably not the best place for me to explore in this instance in any case. Whatever was going on—if indeed there *was* something going on beyond those more visceral sources referred to earlier—seemed, felt, more recent. I was about to step down as chair of my department. Our oldest daughter would soon be getting married. Our other daughter had landed back at home, after having been away for a spell, and that would no doubt create some significant challenges. Things could sometimes be difficult with my wife. Two of my closest friends had suffered mightily around this time, and I had been alongside them, or had tried to be, in whatever way I could. I was beginning to find the professorial life more alienating, and I had begun to think about retirement. The wider world—especially the one created by our lunatic ex-president and his sycophantic acolytes—often seems utterly bathed in bizarre and downright evil stuff, surely enough in itself to make one scream or weep. It couldn't be any one of things—or at least I don't think it could. Was it all of them, conspiring with one another in some sort of unconscious, behind-the-scenes psychic stew, their collective weight having fallen upon me? Or was something else altogether going on? (*What?*)

I should also ask: Where are all of these questions coming from? What kind of person asks them? Among other places, they are coming from a modern western self, the kind of self who asks just these sorts of questions, seeing in the twists and turns of their history the surest sources of being (Gusdorf, 1980 [1956]; Weintraub, 1975). Does this mean that, in the end, all we have are sense-making devices—biophysical, psychoanalytic, Eriksonian-style psychosocial speculations (etc.)—and that, consequently, it's culturally constructed interpretation and narrative "all the way down," pick the one(s) that suit you best?

Thus far I have been talking about events and concrete happenings. Determining how these affect us is difficult in its own right. In fact, strictly speaking, it's impossible. All we have are possibilities, possible ties, linkages—no more, no less. When it comes to broader historical and cultural forces, the interpretive challenge intensifies. Right now, all of us are inhabiting a particular historical and cultural surround at a particular point in time—and we have been doing so throughout the whole of our lives. How does all of *this* affect us? Not unlike my daughter's fall or my dad's death, *that* it gets played out in some way seems unquestionable. But once again, it's extremely difficult to say how.

I spoke of the "wider world" before, and mentioned our lunatic ex-president and his acolytes. Add to this the insurrection of January 6, 2021; the continued violence being perpetrated against Blacks, Jews, Asian-Americans, members of the LGBTQ community, and more; catastrophic climate events; COVID; the war in Ukraine; and on and on and on, virtually all of which has been filtered through the media. All of these realities are now a part of us—or at least those of us who have lived, and are continuing to live, in and through them. They are a part of what I have come to call the "narrative unconscious" (Freeman, 2002a, 2010, 2018a), which comprises those culturally saturated dimensions of history to which we belong and about which we may, once again, be largely unaware. They are working behind the scenes of consciousness, and, like the events and experiences of the personal past, are inevitably leaving their traces within us. But it is no easy task to say, with any specificity, how. Indeed, and again, strictly speaking, it is patently impossible.

Given the language I have been using in this chapter, especially the language of the "impossible," it may seem that the project in which I am engaged is one great big exercise in futility. There is no need to see it this way at all. On the contrary, what I most want to highlight in this chapter, in a different way than in the previous one, is the mystery of who we are and the fact that there is no getting around the open-endedness and unfinalizability of the process of making sense of ourselves. Too often, in psychology, there have been efforts to erase this mystery, or at least subdue it. Issues of meaning and interpretation therefore get shunted aside and attention is directed instead to those facets of behavior and experience that are discrete and containable by whatever measures as might be applied. The fact that we cannot contain and encapsulate much of behavior and experience in this manner and that, consequently, we can "only" interpret, however, far from being a matter of failure, instead underscores what an incredible challenge, and privilege, it is to begin to fathom who and what we are and how we might have gotten that way.

There will be no definitive answers to many of the questions we might wish to pose. I find this to be profoundly humbling and, in a way, beautiful. We are open works, characterized by a profusion of meaning and interpretive possibilities. Perhaps this is what scares people away from the challenge at hand—or leads them to assume that, in the end, any and all interpretations we might arrive at cannot help but be "merely subjective." That subjectivity is involved in the process of interpretation goes without saying; there simply is no view from nowhere, and there is no avoiding our own participation, our own hermeneutical belonging. But this need not lead to the conclusion that our interpretations are merely subjective or that the process is ultimately arbitrary or that every interpretation is as valid as any other.

In many ways, we humans, as open works, are like works of literature: open, filled with meaning, and less amenable to definitive explanation than to interpretive understanding. But some interpretations of such works are surely, and obviously, more valid than others. There are some things that *King Lear*, for instance, is simply not about. There can also be interpretations that are too simplistic or reductive or that fail to take into account central features of the story. Moreover, there are others that (dare I say) are much closer to, and more faithful to, what is actually there, in the text. So, if there is an irreducible multivocality or "plurivocity" to a text, it is, referring to Paul Ricoeur (1973), a *specific* plurivocity, a bounded plurivocity.

Let me flesh out these ideas by turning to some of Hans-Georg Gadamer's work. In an (1979 [1963]) essay titled "The Problem of Historical Consciousness," Gadamer seeks to provide a "sketch of the foundations of a hermeneutic." As he acknowledges, "Historical knowledge cannot be described according to the model of an objectivist knowledge because it is itself a process with all the characteristics of an historical event" (p. 145). He thus considers objectivism an "illusion." He also acknowledges the well-known idea of the hermeneutical circle, which concerns "the circular relation between the whole and its parts: the anticipated meaning of a whole is understood through its parts, but it is in light of the whole that the parts take on their illuminating function" (p. 146). As he goes on to elaborate,

> As soon as he discovers some initially understandable elements, the interpreter sketches out the meaning of the whole text. But these first meaningful elements only come to the fore provided that he sets about reading with a more or less definite interest. Understanding the "thing" which arises there, before him, is nothing less than elaborating a preliminary project which will be progressively corrected in the course of the interpretative reading.
>
> (pp. 148–149)

This process does run the risk of being merely subjective: "One who follows this course always risks falling under the suggestion of his own rough drafts"; in other words, "he runs the risk that the anticipations which he has prepared may not conform to what the thing is." For Gadamer, therefore, "the constant task of understanding lies in the elaboration of projects that are authentic and more proportionate to its object" (pp. 149–150).

Some of what Gadamer has to say may sound surprisingly objectifying, even positivistic, in a way.

> But do not make me say what I have not in fact said; and I have *not* said that when we listen to someone or when we read we ought to forget about our own opinions or shield ourselves against forming an anticipatory idea about the content of the communication. In reality, to be open to "other people's opinions," to a text, and so forth, implies right off that they are *situated* in my system of opinions, or better, that I situate myself in relation to them.
>
> (p. 151)

Now, "it is of course true . . . that other people's opinions"—as well as literary texts—"can have 'in themselves' an indefinite manifold of different meanings . . .; *in concreto*, however, when we listen to someone or read a text we discriminate, from our own standpoint, among the different possible meanings—namely, what *we* consider possible—and we reject the remainder which to us is 'unquestionably absurd'" (p. 151). And so, Gadamer continues,

> The authentic intention of understanding . . . is this: in reading a text, in wishing to understand it, what we always expect is that it will *inform* of us something. A consciousness formed by the authentic hermeneutical attitude will be receptive to the origins and entirely foreign features of that which comes to it from outside its own horizons. Yet this receptivity was not acquired with an objectivist "neutrality"; it is neither possible, necessary, nor desirable that we put ourselves within brackets. The hermeneutical attitude supposes only that we self-consciously designate our opinions and prejudices and qualify them as such, and in so doing strip them of their extreme character. In keeping to this attitude we grant the text the opportunity to appear as an authentically different being and to manifest its own truth, over and against our preconceived notions.
>
> (p. 152)

This is no mere subjectivism or relativism, for what we see in this passage is that the main emphasis is not on the meaning-making process of the interpreter, but on the otherness of the text, its existence as an "authentically different being," able to enlarge us as readers.

What about those situations in which there *is* no "text," no discrete "thing," to constrain and push back against our own preconceptions? Even if we are *like* literary texts in some ways, we are not them. Indeed, when it comes to self-interpretation, much of what we seek to interpret is a constellation of meaning that, on some level, we ourselves have fashioned, in and through memory and imagination. What can it possibly mean, then, to grant the "text" that is ourselves "the opportunity to appear as an authentically different being and to manifest its own truth, over and against our preconceived notions"? We will explore these quite vexing questions in due time. For now, let us acknowledge and appreciate the need for being interpretively humble as we seek to make sense of the human world. This too is cause for wonder—at the fact that we are more than we could ever know and that the interpretive process is bound to be with us until the end of our days.

3 Reverence for the Real

Important though they are for the present inquiry, we are not quite ready to address the questions posed at the close of the previous chapter. For the time being, then, let me work toward establishing the philosophical ground of the perspective I will eventually advance in order to answer them by taking a step back from Gadamer and turning instead to Heidegger, arguably his philosophical forerunner. Here, I pose other questions pertinent to the previous two chapters: How did the kind of ontological brazenness and, at times, arrogance discussed in Chapter 1 come to be? And how did the "squeamishness" about interpretation discussed in Chapter 2 come to be? More generally, how did the objectivity/subjectivity and truth/falsity binaries come to be, with the result that overt behaviors, neurotransmitters, and so on came to be seen as more real than thoughts, minds, and selves? And, returning to Midgley (2014), how did science come to be seen, by many, as the undisputed "victor" in the project of discerning and theorizing reality, thereby leading to the scientism we too often see? As Midgley is quick to insist, rightly,

> perhaps we can never feel too much reverence for science, or for any branch of knowledge. Knowledge is indeed wonderful and should be revered. Scientism's mistake does not lie in over-praising one form of it, but in cutting that form off from the rest of thought, in treating it as a victor who has put all the rest out of business.
>
> (p. 5)

Even physical science ought not to be seen as "a separate, supreme champion outclassing history or philosophy" (p. 6). . . . Today," however, Midgley continues, "Science [note the capital S she has now affixed to the term] tends to be exalted in isolation, as if any attempt to relate it to other valuable activities was anti-scientific" (p. 7). This perspective is nothing less than a "myth," pejoratively understood, and as those of us who may try to counter this myth in the classroom well know, it is not easily dispelled. One reason is that "it is at present being propounded by actual scientists: people with appropriate PhDs who work in labs, some of them indeed very distinguished." This can

DOI: 10.4324/9780429323652-4

lead to an uncritical reverence on the part of students, especially; they can be shocked by the "fact" of their own apparent illusions and in awe of the scientists who, in the name of Reality and Truth, serve as the demystifiers. "There is no mind, no self, no God? Who knew?!" Putting aside the potential recklessness of this sort of scientism, we also see that "science education has of late become very narrow. It doesn't direct people's attention half-enough to understanding the meaning of what they are saying, in particular to the difference between our various ways of thinking. And what it hardly ever teaches them is to take notice of those deep assumptions" undergirding the perspective; "they are simply taken for granted" (p. 8). "Of course psychology is a science! Of course it relies on *the* scientific method! Of course it seeks to objectify and quantify and build theories based on the findings yielded! What else could it be?" What else indeed. . . . Psychology thus becomes a "hyperscience," as Thomas Teo (2020) has called it, seeking to colonize the whole of human reality. I ask again: How did all this come to be? And how might we begin to think beyond it?

Because I have been trying to write this book in the common tongue, or at least something close to it, I hesitate to do a deep dive into some of Heidegger's thinking, but I really must. For the sake of brevity and accessibility, I will turn my attention to the essay "Science and reflection" (1977), which, for me, has become something of a go-to answer to this very question. In doing so, I draw liberally on my own (Freeman, 2007a, 2007b) account of the essay. "Regarded in terms of its essence," Heidegger writes, "the reality within which man of today moves and attempts to maintain himself is, with regard to its fundamental characteristics, determined on an increasing scale by and in conjunction with that which we call Western European science" (p. 156). Indeed, he continues, "When we ponder this ongoing event, it becomes evident that in the Western world and during the eras of its history, science has developed such a power as could never have been met with on the earth before, and that consequently this power is ultimately to be spread over the entire globe" (p. 156). These are strong words: Science—modern science—is a monolith, powerful in its reach. How shall this monolith be characterized? "*Science*," Heidegger answers, "*is the theory of the real*" (p. 157).

For this proclamation to have any meaning, it will be important to unpack its key terms: "real" and "theory." It will also be necessary to show how these two terms are related to one another. Only then, Heidegger suggests, will we find ourselves in the position of seeing more clearly modern science's essential features and, for present purposes, the resultant truth/falsity binary that has been perpetuated.

We begin with the term "real," which, especially in the time of the ancient Greeks, Heidegger tells us, had a far more expansive meaning than it currently has, connoting something that emerges, is "unconcealed," brought forth out of hiddenness or dormancy. Eventually (and to make a quite long story short), the meaning of the real changes, morphing into something closer to the factual, which "today connotes assurance, and means the same thing as 'certain' and 'sure'." As such, "it is neither an accident nor a harmless caprice in the change of meaning of mere terms that, since the beginning of the modern period in the seventeenth century, the word 'real' has meant the same thing as 'certain'" (pp. 161–162). In a distinct sense, the factual, one might say, became mistaken for the real, such that the nonfactual, in turn, came to be seen as unreal, fictitious, and possibly flat-out *false*. "The 'real'," therefore, "in the sense of what is factual," Heidegger continues, "now constitutes the opposite of that which does not stand firm as guaranteed and which is represented as mere appearance or as something that is only believed to be so." The real never becomes *only* this, he clarifies; "throughout these various changes in meaning the real still retains the more primordially fundamental characteristic, which comes less often and differently to the fore, of something that presences which sets itself forth from out of itself" (1977, p. 162). Nevertheless, there is a process of delimitation that (ostensibly) occurred, with the result that the "more primordially fundamental characteristic"—*out of which the factually real emerges*—progressively becomes relegated to the background, such that the real "appears in the modern age as object" (p. 163) and comes to be associated with the raw, brute stuff of the world, uninterpreted and unconstructed.

In addition, the real becomes associated with the *now*, the immediate, that which is sensuously present. The real, in other words, comes to be tied essentially to *clock* time, the time of lines, sequences, and moments, strung along like beads. There is a twofold problem here relevant to the concerns I seek to address in this chapter. By virtue of the delimitation of the real to the realm of "objectness," phenomena that cannot readily be encapsulated as objects—such as personal narratives—frequently come to be seen as *un*real, or as fictions or even lies, imposed upon all of the brute data to give them some form and order. Second, by virtue of the associated delimitation of time to clock time, other modes of time—such as lived time or what has been called *narrative* time (Ricoeur, 1981a)—progressively become seen as too fleeting, and too subjective, to have much commerce with reality. The result is that there emerges a conception of reality and of time that is much more readily applied to the world of *things* than to the world of *people* (Freeman, 2003).

It is at this juncture that Heidegger can ask: "What is the real in relation to theory, and thus in a certain respect also in and through theory?" In accordance with the earlier, Greek meaning of the "real," "theory" had been understood to involve a process of "[looking] attentively on the outward appearance wherein what presences becomes visible and through such sight—seeing—to linger with it" (p. 163). Or, as Heidegger puts the matter shortly after, theory—*theōria*—had been seen as "the reverent paying heed to the unconcealment of what presences" (p. 164). In modern parlance, it might be related to the kind of attentive beholding frequently associated with mindfulness or meditative illumination. This too changed, however, such that "there comes to the fore the impulse, already prepared in Greek thinking, of a looking-at that sunders and compartmentalizes" (p. 166). Rather than mindfulness or illumination, therefore, we come to have *observation*. "Theory," in turn, becomes "the viewing, the observation, of the real" (p. 166)—or, more specifically, "an entrapping and securing refining of the real." Heidegger puts the matter as follows:

> Science sets upon the real. It orders it into place to the end that at any given time the real will exhibit itself as an interacting network, i.e., in a surveyable series of related causes. The real thus becomes surveyable and capable of being followed out in its sequences. The real becomes secured in its objectness. From this there result spheres or areas of objects that scientific observation can entrap after its fashion. Entrapping representation, which secures everything in that objectness which is thus capable of being followed out, is the fundamental characteristic of the representing through which modern sciences corresponds to the real.
>
> (p. 168)

This view of theory, Heidegger goes on to note, "would have been as strange to medieval man as it would have been dismaying to Greek thought" (p. 168). Scientific theory is to "entrap" the real as it is "followed out in its sequences" and must thus entail modes of representation that adequately embody this theoretical commitment.

But there is still more to the transformation Heidegger is seeking to document. As Max Planck (cited by Heidegger) once stated, and as much of contemporary social science would likewise maintain, "That is real which can be measured." This criterion is perhaps a bit looser than some of the others that have been identified. Some scientists would argue this, others not. In either case, we can certainly say that the "surveyability" that science seeks is frequently manifested in the demand for quantification and always manifested in the demand for what might be termed "representational precision." The result of all of this: Research Methods and Statistics!

This brings us to another, deeper problem, having to do with the discourse of causality and, in a related vein, the task of "surveying" just considered. As Heidegger notes, in many forms of science, the relationship between variables will be charted in a sequential, "if-then" fashion—which is to say, in accordance with clock time. In psychology, hard and fast if-then relationships of this sort are notoriously difficult to come by. As such, they are often substituted by "if-*probably* then" relationships, that is, statistical ones. In both cases, the arrow of time moves essentially forward, the fundamental supposition being that the temporality of antecedent and consequence is intrinsic to the scientific endeavor. This perspective has its place, in psychology and beyond. But it is hardly the only way to conceptualize psychological inquiry. Indeed, as I suggested earlier, when I noted that this forward-looking view entails a conception of reality and of time that is more readily applied to the world of things than to the world of people, this perspective occludes other modes of considering reality and time, include narrative time, which essentially involves looking backward over the landscape of the past, from the vantage point of the present, in order to discern patterns of meaning that can only be gleaned retrospectively, via memory and narrative (Carr, 1986; Danto, 1985; Kerby, 1991; Ricoeur, 1981a; Taylor, 1989).

There is much more that might be said about this particular set of issues, but let us return to Heidegger and the broader constellation of issues he is exploring. If Heidegger is right, there is something "concealed" in the view of science understood as the theory of the real. What is it? "Theory identifies the real . . . and fixes it into *one* object-area." However, "Theory never outstrips nature . . . and in this sense theory never makes its way around nature" (p. 173). As Heidegger continues, "Scientific representation is never able to encompass the coming to presence of nature; for the objectness of nature is, antecedently, only *one* way in which nature exhibits itself" (p. 174). Heidegger is discussing physics at this juncture of the essay, and his point is a relatively simple one. Physics does not, and cannot, deal with the "whole" of nature but only a portion of it. "Nature thus remains for the science of physics that which cannot be gotten around" (p. 174). We can say much the same thing of that phenomenon we might simply call a "life": It too remains that which cannot be gotten around. It is the backdrop against which much of psychology moves, and it is what remains after that which can be objectified is secured through observation and theory.

As Heidegger notes, one might expect "that science itself could find present within itself that which is not to be gotten around, and could define it as such." That is to say, one might assume that it ought to be able to look beyond its own borders, to see what is there beyond the realm of circumscribable objects. "But it is precisely this," he insists,

> that does not come about, and indeed because anything like it is essentially impossible. What is the basis for our knowing this? If the sciences themselves should at any time be able to find at hand within themselves what is not to be gotten around of which we are speaking, they would have before all else to be in a position to conceive and represent their own essence.
>
> (p. 176)

However, they are "never in a position to do this" and are thus "utterly incapable of gaining access to that which is not to be gotten around holding sway in their essence" (p. 177).

This brings us to a most curious, and ironic, state of affairs: In a certain sense, Heidegger seems to agree with those gatekeepers, mentioned earlier, who say that science is *this* rather than *that*—that is, that it *cannot* "by definition" deal with reality in its fullness but rather only that which can be secured as object. Science, in other words, from this perspective, simply cannot do justice to this fullness, this *surplus*, by its very nature. That which is not to be gotten around therefore remains behind the scenes: "What is inaccessible and not to be gotten around remains in inconspicuousness," and for this reason is "constantly passed over." This, again, is why the deeper regions of being are frequently left to poets and philosophers, those who are less entrapped by their own rules and procedures—or, more positively, those who seek to practice greater fidelity to the fullness of reality. But these regions can, and should, be part of psychology, or at least that sector of it that seeks to maintain a substantial space for that which is not to be gotten around. The reason, in short: *Reality requires it*, and there is no inherent reason for psychologists to exempt themselves from the endeavor. Reality also requires *reverence* and not only the control and entrapment and domination that so pervades the hyperscientific quarters of the discipline. This reverence for the real may be seen as a critical feature of the psychological humanities as envisioned herein.

None of what has been said thus far is intended to indict or invalidate the psychology-as-science idea. If Heidegger is right, though, the sciences have emerged out of something more primordial, and what they exclude and render inaccessible is, in reality, their very source and ground. I think Heidegger is basically right in offering this rendition of science. We must nevertheless ask: Must it be this way? More specifically, is it possible to *rethink* the meaning of science itself in such a way as to include at least some of what it has heretofore rendered inaccessible? Hard-nosed types may say no; it is what it is. For different reasons, Heidegger might say something similar; again, it is not within the purview of science to see beyond its own borders. By his own admission, however, the science that Heidegger discusses throughout this essay "always refers exclusively to the new science of modern times" (p. 157). It does not, in other words, refer to what science *can* be or *ought* to be, only to what it *is*, in the modern age. We can therefore refine the question at hand: Must science be what it currently is? The answer to this question is surely no; the meaning of science has changed and will no doubt continue to change as time passes. The question then becomes: Is there any compelling reason for rethinking the scientific enterprise articulated as "the theory of the real"? More to the point still, is there any compelling reason to rethink the essence of modern science?

I think there is, and it has to do with practicing *fidelity* to the phenomena. The first requirement of science, I maintain, is to be faithful to the phenomena—even when they are as complex, ambiguous, and downright messy as a human life. Precisely because of this complexity, ambiguity, and messiness, I have suggested, much of contemporary social science, psychology especially, has opted for safer, more discrete objects, ones that lend themselves to objectification, quantification, replication, and all the rest. This, again, is fine: There are without question aspects of human reality that can be isolated in this way, and doing so can be most productive. The problem, therefore, isn't so much what psychology *does*, which has its own sphere of validity, but what it *doesn't* do and what it claims it *can't* and *shouldn't* do. For, insofar as psychological science promotes the view that reality is coextensive with that which can be secured as object, it will, of necessity, have promoted a radically restricted image of the human condition. Put more simply, it will not have been *faithful* to the human condition and will therefore have *violated*, violently, the first call of science. Why "violently"? It will have excised, cut off, some of those very features that render human reality *human* and thereby *dehumanized* the very being it sought to understand, turned it into an object and imagined that its objectness exhausted its realness. In this respect, it might be suggested, contemporary psychological science is not nearly scientific enough.

What, then, is to be done? How is "science" to be rethought? Among other requirements, it would need to employ a kind of language that move beyond the entrapping, objectifying language that characterizes much of psychology. How might such a language emerge? And what sort of "attitude" might it require? Beginning with the latter first, the attitude Heidegger refers to requires *reflection*, which he takes to be "calm, self-possessed surrender to that which is worthy of questioning" (p. 180). The aforementioned term "reverence"—which Heidegger had framed as "the reverent paying heed to the unconcealment of what presences"—fits nicely here too. It is reverence for the fullness of reality. In regard to the language appropriate to such reverence, it must be *poetic*, broadly conceived (Heidegger, 1971). It will be a language that aims more to suggest, express, and evoke than to argue and convince, and it will seek to open a "region" of truth, as I have called it (Freeman, 2002c, 2010), rather than pretend to present a definitive one. Its foremost aim, through it all, will be to practice fidelity to the real and to do so reflectively, with an abiding, perhaps gentle, reverence.

As with all explorations that seek to contribute in some way to science, there needs to be rigor and precision of thought. There also needs to be, in the case of the written word, a good measure of writerliness, the capacity to use language artfully. Why? Consider the poet in this context: Through their words, some feature of reality may be brought to light, unconcealed, and the degree to which this occurs is a function of the degree to which the poet can employ language, artfully, in service of the task. We therefore arrive at what might seem, on the face of it, a "strange," even contradictory, conclusion: *the more art, the more science*. In other words, the more poetically charged and inspired the work, the closer it may be to the phenomena themselves and the more likely it would be that the resultant account would be scientifically valid and significant. Along these lines, I have suggested that language of this sort might be oriented not only toward *thinking* but *feeling* and that, in addition to supporting the customary *epistemological* aim of increasing knowledge and understanding of the human realm, it can support the *ethical* aim of increasing sympathy and compassion (Freeman, 2000, 2011, 2018a). It can also provide readers the opportunity for much the same kind of felt engagement that works of literature can provide when they seek to reveal the deeper realities of people's lives. Hence the need for what I have called *poetic science* (Freeman, 2007a, 2011).

Just in case this sounds too much like aestheticism, plain and simple, or that it appears to blunt the sort of critical edge that is often sought in the social sciences, I believe this critical edge remains very much in the picture. My takeoff point here is a little book written some time ago by Herbert Marcuse called *The Aesthetic Dimension* (1978), in which he tries to identify some of the shortcomings of Marxist aesthetics by focusing on the liberating moment of the aesthetic itself. "Under the law of aesthetic form," he writes, "the given reality is necessarily *sublimated*: the immediate content is stylized, the 'data' are reshaped and reordered in accordance with the demands of the art form. . . . Aesthetic sublimation," Marcuse continues, "makes for the affirmative, reconciling component of art, though it is at the same time a vehicle for the critical, negating function of art." This critical function "resides in the aesthetic form. . . . The work of art thus re-presents reality while accusing it" (pp. 7–8). In short, "The truth of art lies in its power to break the monopoly of established reality (i.e., of those who established it) to *define* what is *real*" (p. 9). This brings us all the way back to the notion of science as "the theory of the real." Psychological inquiry, or at least a portion of it, conceived as poetic science, bears within it the potential to not only redefine *science* but *reality* itself.

Ironically enough, it is against the background of these ideas and ideals that some—including some qualitative researchers themselves—suggest that their work has little to do with the real: because it moves beyond the kind of visibility/observability frequently associated with the "real stuff," real *data*, and because it may not lend itself to quantification, it may be understood as purely, or essentially, "subjective." I want to flip this idea, and suggest instead that, in contemporary psychology especially, what frequently is touted as *objective* is actually more *subjective*, and what is frequently decried as *subjective* is actually more *objective*. I remember feeling this acutely back in grad school when I first encountered a great big correlation matrix. We, members of the research team, stood around the pale green and white printouts excitedly waiting to see where the significant correlations were, and with those in hand, we tried to craft a picture of what might be going on. The entire process was utterly speculative and was more about our assumptions than anything else. I eventually rejected doing this sort of work, at least on that particular project, much to the chagrin of my superiors. Instead, I wanted to pursue in-depth life histories, some of which turned out to be 100 pages long, and deal with them interpretively, hermeneutically. And that was seen to be a more subjective approach! The irony is stunning, truly.

One way to think and speak about what I am proposing in this chapter is to posit what might be called an *objectivity before objectivity*—by which I mean a form of objectivity that *precedes* those more objectifying forms that have come to be enshrined in social science, especially psychology. Iris Murdoch gives us some helpful words for moving in the direction I'm outlining here. "We are anxiety-ridden animals," she (1970) writes. "Our minds are continually active, fabricating an anxious, usually self-preoccupied, often falsifying veil which partially conceals the world" (p. 84). Objectivity, Murdoch-style, therefore, has to do with our capacity to "unself" ourselves, as she puts it, to resist our own egocentric fantasies and reveries and to thereby see what is really there, before us. We can extend this idea in the present context by saying that it has to do with our capacity to resist those objectifying schemes that occlude, rather than reveal, reality. I have already suggested that much of psychology employs just these sorts of schemes, such that there results a kind of *faux* objectivity, or *pseudo*-objectivity. If Murdoch, and Heidegger before her, is right, there is a deeper form of it, one that entails a kind of mindful beholding of whatever comes before us, no matter how messy, elusive, and ungraspable it may be.

I remain attracted to the term "poetic science" and to the idea it embodies insofar as it leads to a view of science that is not only more capacious and inclusive but also aspires to be more faithful to the phenomena of interest, especially those that have traditionally been deemed too recalcitrant to be welcomed into the hallowed halls of psychology. It is for this reason that I found myself questioning Heidegger's assertion that science "is what it is" [*not* his words] and that, consequently, the challenge of dealing with "that which is not to be gotten around" must lead us to turn elsewhere. That seemed to me to be giving up the game, and I saw no reason why science "had" to assume the form it had, particularly in psychology. I still hold to this basic idea, and if truth be told, if I were a young psychologist, seeking gainful employment or tenure, I might still try to put forth this reimagined version of science, if only to be able to proclaim: I'm part of the club too. I do science; it's just a different brand than the most of you practice. Let us live together peacefully.

It's quite possible that some readers, including those later in their careers, who have little to lose in terms of job possibilities, tenure, and so on, will continue to carry out their inquiries under the august mantle of science and will continue to work toward a view of the psychological sciences that is more inclusive and welcoming, in the way I have described. That's cool; we all have our predilections, and I have no interest whatsoever in indicting this sort of commitment. But I myself have come to ask a question that, curiously enough, eluded me, or remained dormant, for many years: *Must* psychology continue to be framed as a science? How come? More sophomorically still: Who says?

Well, some may respond, the APA says, and the APS, and all of those Intro textbooks out there, and all of psychology's heroes, strenuously committed as they were to lift the discipline out of the dark dungeon of prescientific speculation into the light of modernity. But there is simply no inherent need to frame things this way. This is the negative, critical moment of my "realization": No;

there is no transcendental, *a priori* ground for the commitment disciplinary psychology made. But as I hope has become clearer through this chapter along with the first two, there was, there is, a positive, constructive moment to the realization too: There are regions of human life that demand something else, something more attentive and attuned to those realities of human experience that elude or exceed the grasp of science, at least as traditionally conceived. This something is the psychological humanities. Let us therefore explore more deeply the rationale for this turn and why it is a critically important one for the discipline.

4 Reaching for the Poetic

In the previous chapter, I noted that, "curiously enough," the question of why psychology had to be deemed a science had eluded me for some time. Why "curiously enough"? It's because I had been doing humanities-oriented work for nearly 40 years, beginning with the very first pieces I wrote (Freeman, 1984, 1985a, 1985b). It's curious that I didn't quite see it. Actually, though, it really isn't so curious, for the pressure to stay the scientific course—or to at least say I did—was pretty mighty. Forgive me if some readers have heard these two brief stories before, but I feel compelled to tell them again (see also Freeman, 2014b).

Here is the first one. The year was 1996 and the event was the Psi Chi (National Honor Society for Psychology in the United States) induction ceremony at Holy Cross, for some odd reason I was the featured speaker, and I was determined to speak my piece on behalf of qualitative, and especially narrative, inquiry. In fact, what I proposed in the talk, titled "Narrative Psychology and the Study of Human Lives (Or, the Importance of Category C)," was that qualitative inquiry needed to be considered as integral a part of our department's curriculum as all the rest. "After many, many years and many false starts," I said, "psychology is finally arriving at an appropriate way of speaking about the human realm." This language, I proclaimed (somewhat self-servingly), was tied to the idea of narrative, which I described as "the interpretive study of human lives, in their 'natural habitats' (as in 'real life' rather than the lab); in time (that is, over the course of time); and, finally, in culture." It's possible that some of my colleagues were with me, in a "maybe this makes sense" way. "Just in case some of you out there think this new movement is a fantasy construction of mine," I continued, "I might note that there are actually a whole lot of 'name brand' psychologists—Jerome Bruner, Carol Gilligan, and others—who are moving in this direction, seeing in the idea of narrative an important inroad into issues that, for too long, have fallen outside the scope of 'legitimate' psychology." Name brand psychologists, of course, don't necessarily translate into good psychology, I acknowledged; sometimes it's just the opposite. "But in this case," I said, "I'm convinced that there is more real momentum in this area of the discipline than there has ever been before. . . . I won't be so audacious as to claim that it's *the* wave of the future. But it's almost certainly *a* wave."

DOI: 10.4324/9780429323652-5

And on I went, trying to tell everyone what it meant to ride the wave and how it might transform not only our department but the entire discipline: "Holy Cross, in its own modest way"—it seemed like a bit of modesty was in order—"has the potential to become something of a leader in charting this new area of psychology," partly because there were a couple of other people doing qualitative work in the department but mainly because "we're in the process of actually making these issues a regular part of our curriculum." At the time, the curriculum consisted of Introductory Psychology, Statistics, Research Methods, History and Systems of Psychology, and selections from what was called "Category A," which covered psychology as a natural science (through courses such as Physiological Psychology, Learning, Sensation and Perception, and Cognition and Memory), and "Category B," psychology as a social science (through courses such as Social Psychology, Abnormal Psychology, Developmental Psychology, and Personality). Well, I asked, "What, if anything, is left? That is, what remains of structured psychological interest after we've subtracted Category A and B phenomena?" The answer was clear: "What remains . . . is the living, breathing, loving, suffering, praying, dying human being. Or, to put the matter another way, what remains is precisely the being who learns, senses and perceives, thinks and remembers, who develops a personality and is engaged socially, with others, and occasionally behaves in somewhat abnormal fashion. Or, to put the matter another way yet again—and to return to the definition I offered earlier—what we're talking about here are human lives, real human lives, existing in time and in culture." And so, it was high time to launch Category C: psychology as a human science. I then went on to describe both the defining features of the category and the kinds of courses that would likely fall under it. The students were excited, as they generally are in these kinds of situations; what I was describing to them is what they had once thought psychology was actually about. A few of my colleagues seemed interested too. I had made the whole thing seem so cutting-edge, humane, and, not least, Holy Cross-compatible (we take pride in emphasizing our commitment to "the whole person," engaging students in "basic human questions," and so on), that the entire performance seemed to emerge as a truly winning one—until the very end, when a well-respected colleague came up to me, expressed some appreciation for what I had said, and then asked, "Why do you call yourself a psychologist?" And what, did any of it have to do with *science*?

Here's the second story. It was some years later, I had put myself up for full professor, and the day had come for me to receive my department report. I wasn't particularly frightened at the prospect; knowing that most of my colleagues probably hadn't read what I had written but saw that it was somehow getting published, I figured things would go okay. Then I received the report, and what the cover letter said was that my colleagues very much enjoyed reading my work but had absolutely no way of gauging its value for psychology and that, consequently, they had passed my dossier on to the English

Department, who would undoubtedly be able to make better sense of things than they could. *What?!* Just kidding, the person who gave me the letter said. My departmental colleagues were more playful this time around, but the question being posed was much the same. Why do you call yourself a psychologist? And what place does your work have in psychological science, if any?

I wasn't at all prepared for the first encounter. The second I was able to brush off as a (more or less) good-natured, teasing gesture. Now that I have had the time to really digest these questions, however, I believe I am better prepared to provide a serviceable answer—or at least the one I would have wanted to provide back then if I had really wanted to engage them in the issues at hand. It would have gone something like this: "*I'm* the one who's doing true science here! Not, of course, the kind of (objectifying, reductive, positivistic) science you've been reared on but one that's much more adequate to the phenomena we're (supposedly) interested in learning about! In fact," I might have gone on to say, "the promise of qualitative/Category C inquiry is that it can lead to the *self-realization* of psychology itself—that is, the coming-into-being of its distinctive potential as an arena of scientific inquiry" (see Freeman, 2014b). After putting forth this audacious assertion, I would almost certainly have had to explain myself. *"You?"* they might have said. "True science? Self-realization of the discipline? What *on earth* are you talking about?" "Well," I might have responded, "let me begin by offering a premise that undergirds much of what I have to say, and that is that much of the work that gets done in psychology, in its aim of being scientifically objective, actually ends up distorting the phenomena and in this sense ends up being *less*, rather than more, faithful to reality." There would likely have been some measure of confusion at this point if not outright disdain: "What *we* do is objective," our colleagues may say. "What *you* do is clearly not." Operating from the framework of mainstream psychological inquiry, there is some justification for them saying so. But as we saw in the previous chapter, the conception of objectivity from which they are working needs to be interrogated, radically.

I might have even thrown in a watered-down version of Heidegger (1977) at this point, telling them, cautiously, that time was when the "real" connoted just the sort of fullness and plenitude that many of us would associate with the fabric of human lives and that eventually, its meaning would change, moving in a much more discrete, circumscribable direction. What we therefore find in a good portion of social scientific inquiry as we approach the modern era (I might have gone on to "explain") is the idea that we achieve the greatest degree of objectivity by limiting the objects of interest to the most containable and measurable. So, isn't it time that we started doing some *true* science rather than the *faux* science we've been bequeathed? (It's wise that I didn't do this.)

Now, though, my response would be somewhat different—and there is a chance that some of my colleagues even know this. In keeping with what has been said thus far, it would be that it is high time for psychology to break out of its unnecessarily constrictive scientific cocoon, spread its wings, and embrace the arts and humanities, not just as helpful resources for our various projects but as full-fledged players in the discipline. For the sake of keeping the peace, I would no doubt quickly go on to say, "I'm not suggesting that we ought to replace psychological science with the arts and humanities! What you all do is significant and valuable! Please keep doing it! Let a thousand flowers bloom!" (This would actually be somewhat disingenuous. A good deal of what gets done in psychology is not particularly significant or valuable; some of it, I believe, is positively trivial and wasteful.) The other thing I might say is: "Truthfully, I don't really care what this enterprise I've been talking is called. There's a good deal of arbitrariness in how things are defined, and whether we call this animal science or something else is largely irrelevant." Philosophically speaking, I believe this. Practically speaking, though, I think that finding a new and improved language for speaking to what some of us are doing is vitally important, partly because it can serve to "formally" legitimize what is already being done and partly—and more importantly—because it can open up modes and lines of inquiry that have heretofore been closed. After all, I might conclude, "Don't we all want the most open, flexible, creative, wide-ranging discipline we could possibly have, one that can serve as an unparalleled exemplar of the full range of liberal arts inquiry?" "Hooray!!!" they might scream. "Thank you!" (Unlikely.)

Who knows? Maybe I can share some of these thoughts with them someday. I am pretty close to retirement and there's some attraction to letting them know what I actually think. Time will tell. For the time being, I will continue to direct my words to theoretical and philosophical psychologists, humanistic psychologists, qualitative psychologists, and those other fellow travelers who may be interested. So, let us continue. Here, I will be telling a more explicitly "theoretical" story, drawing especially on two pieces, the first, "Theory beyond theory" (2000), and the second, "Toward a poetics of the Other: New directions in post-scientific psychology" (2019b).

In the first of these pieces (Freeman, 2000), I made significant contact with the philosopher Stephen Toulmin's important book *Cosmopolis: The Hidden Agenda of Modernity* (1990). As Toulmin suggests, the "received view" of modernity, which he traces largely to Descartes and Galileo, brought with it a fourfold transformation: from the oral to the written, from the particular to the universal, from the local to the general, and from the timely to the timeless. On his account, this transformation entailed a movement from the *practical* to the *theoretical*, with "theoretical" essentially referring to that sort of conceptual structuring and even entrapment which we considered, via Heidegger (1977), in the previous chapter. It is exactly this movement that gave us the contours of modern science, in psychology and beyond. The main problem with this view, Toulmin argues, in a variant of Heidegger's thesis, is not only that it was employed to support a highly abstract, decontextualized, rationalistic perspective on inquiry (see especially Slife, 2004; also Fowers, 2005; Gergen, 2009; Kirschner & Martin, 2010; Richardson, 2012 [and many others, too numerous to name here]) but also that it eclipsed and even nullified other possible perspectives. Indeed, one of the main aims of the book was to call attention to the fact that, alongside the Cartesian/Galilean worldview, grounded in natural philosophy, was a quite different one, grounded in Renaissance humanism, most notably in the figure of Montaigne. Toulmin thus spoke of "the dual trajectory of Modernity," his aim being nothing less than to resurrect this buried history and to thereby "reappropriate the reasonable and tolerant (but neglected) legacy of humanism" and "to find ways of moving on from the received view of Modernity—which set the exact sciences and the humanities apart—to a reformed version, which redeems philosophy and science, by reconnecting them to the humanist half of Modernity" (p. 180).

As I have already indicated, I am not sure whether to fully follow Toulmin in this move. With the aforementioned idea of poetic science, I did indeed seek to "restore" to science this eclipsed humanist legacy in order to humanize it. Eventually, however, I came to question this move, and even began to feel that cramming everything under the umbrella of science, however broadly conceived, was disingenuous in a way (Freeman, 2015). Did the work I was doing really warrant being considered science, *however* broadly conceived?

I hope it is clear by now am not interested in science-bashing. Generally speaking, it's foolish and pointless. Nor, however, do I feel the need to kowtow to the scientific project by forcing all the things we more humanistically inclined types do under the umbrella of science. In any case, after fleshing out some preliminary ideas in the (Freeman, 2000) piece, I offered the conviction "that there exists the need for at least a portion of theoretical psychology to move beyond theory—as ordinarily conceived—altogether," that it "simply abandons its commitment to theoretical scientificity and that it become more closely tied to the humanities." The main reason: Exploring the concrete details of practical experience, in the way Toulmin and others (e.g., Nussbaum, 1990) had proposed, pointed in the direction of a very different enterprise, one closer to "poetics" than to "theoretics" (p. 75). I might note that it was also at that juncture that I made one of my first forays into the idea of the "Other," especially as addressed by Emmanuel Levinas (1996, 1999). Why turn to the Other? One reason was Levinas's (1996) insistence on the particularity and irreducibility of the other person. "Concrete reality," he had written, "is man [and woman] always already in relation with the world. These relations cannot be reduced to theoretical representation. The latter would only confirm the autonomy of the thinking subject, . . . the subject closed in on itself" (p. 19). As he puts the matter elsewhere (1985), focusing explicitly on his well-known idea of the *face* of the Other:

> The face is signification, and signification without context. I mean that the Other, in the rectitude of his face, is not a character within a context.

> Ordinarily one is a "character": a professor at the Sorbonne, a Supreme Court justice, son of so-and-so, everything that is in one's passport, the manner of dressing, of presenting oneself. And all signification in the usual sense of the term is relative to such a context: the meaning of something is in its relation to another thing. Here, to the contrary, the face is meaning all by itself. You are you. In this sense one can say that the face is not "seen." It is what cannot become a content, which your thought would embrace; it is uncontainable, it leads you beyond.
>
> (pp. 86–87)

Another reason for turning to the idea of the Other was Levinas's insistence on the primacy of the ethical dimension, the idea that, before there is category, concept and theory, indeed before there is ontology, there is the magnetic pull of the Other, calling me out of myself, beyond myself. "Thinking the other person," he writes,

> is a part of the irreducible concern for the other. Love is not consciousness. It is because there is a vigilance before the awakening that the cogito is possible, so that ethics is before ontology. Before the arrival of the human is already vigilance for the other. The transcendental I in its nakedness comes from the awakening by and for the other.
>
> (1999, p. 98)

A third, and related, reason had to do with Levinas's still broader aim of "thinking Otherwise" (Freeman, 2012) about the human condition, which highlights the importance of psychology moving from its fundamentally ego-centric perspective to a more "ex-centric" perspective, predicated on the magnetic, centrifugal pull of the Other, both human and nonhuman.

By way of summing up the 2000 article, I wrote the following:

> (T)he project of theory, which "entraps the real and secures it in its objectness" (Heidegger, 1977, p. 168), is correlative with the primacy of the sovereign subject, the Cartesian *cogito*, seeking to represent the world qua object, thing, *It*. The displacement of emphasis, from the *cogito* to the Other, in turn, requires the movement beyond theory, toward the poetic, where truth becomes less a matter of adequacy to the object than fidelity—phenomenological *and* ethical—to others, particularly those in need, who call forth our responsiveness and care. Hence the idea of a "poetics of the Other."
>
> (p. 76)

The idea of the Other, I went on to clarify, was not to be restricted to the human other but "may usefully be extended to those nonhuman regions of 'otherness' encountered, for instance, in aesthetic and religious experience as well. These too entail the displacement of the *cogito* and, arguably, require different modes of thinking and writing than those ordinarily associated with theoretical reflection" (p. 76). More on this in Chapter 8.

As for where "theory" fit into this view, I pulled another putatively paradoxical maneuver by underscoring the importance of "theorizing the untheorizable." As George Steiner (1989) had argued, in a manner akin to Heidegger (1977), "The word 'theory' has lost its birthright. At the source, it draws on meanings both secular and ritual" and "tells of concentrated insight, of an act of contemplation focused patiently on its object" (p. 69). This would change in the sixteenth century, "with the inward shift and displacement of understanding into the ego," with the result that the term came to be seen as "a subjective speculative impulse" to be "tested and proved by corresponding facts, by the mirroring evidence of empirical reality" (p. 70). Along the lines being drawn, I might have titled the 2000 piece "Theory *before* theory" rather than "Theory *beyond* theory"—not just for the sake of harking back to an older version of the idea but for the sake of highlighting the *priority* of that sort of patient, Other-directed mindfulness—and reverence—which precedes the kind of speculative formulating that has come to characterize much of the theoretical enterprise.

So, a poetics of the Other, infused by a new/old version of "theory" that would appear to fit well with the project. The article I have been referring to was, in the end, a kind of promissory note—a prolegomenon, as it were, to the larger, more comprehensive work that was to follow it. There have been follow-ups here and there, for instance in *The Priority of the Other* (Freeman, 2014a). But the poetic dimension remained muted in that work. Moreover, and again, I continued to issue the call in that text for "poetic science," my still-remaining assumption being that some measure of scientificity was a requirement. The challenge, therefore, was to find a language that would allow for the possibility for at least a portion of psychology to become truly *other* than what it had been—by reaching more explicitly for the poetic (Freeman, 2018b; Kearney, 1998; Paz, 1967; Ricoeur, 1981b) and by fleshing out the idea of a poetics of the Other (Freeman, 2019a).

In order to begin to make the case, I turn briefly to Toulmin once more, this time to another important work, *Return to Reason* (2001). As Toulmin reminds us, "Not until 1600 A.D. was there any widespread tendency to insist on the superiority of theoretical abstraction and logical deduction, at the expense of directly human modes of analysis" (p. 29). There is no questioning the advantages that accrued from this tendency. But the fact is,

> Problems begin when people forget what limits they accepted in mastering the systematic procedures of their disciplines. Once forgetfulness sets in, the ground is prepared for misunderstandings and cross-purposes: the

> selective attention called for in a disciplined activity is elevated to the status of being "the one and only right way" of performing the tasks in question, and the possibility of approaching them from a different standpoint, or with different priorities, is ignore or, we may say, "bracketed off."
> (p. 42)

Such bracketing off need not be harmful "if it leaves open the possibility of other, alternative procedures: selective attention is one thing, blinders are another" (p. 42). This is the moment of critique I referred to in the previous chapter. I trust that this line of thinking sounds familiar by now.

With this, we can move more squarely in the direction of the positive, constructive moment. According to Toulmin (2001), one of the surest inroads into the kind of practical knowledge he wishes to advance comes in the form of narratives. When considering medicine and certain areas of psychology, such narratives frequently emerge as case histories geared toward addressing specific concerns. "But, when a clinician's attention widens to embrace things about a patient that go beyond these concerns, and faces human experience as a patient lives it, the resulting narratives are more like those we look for in the writings of biographers and even novelists" (p. 125; see also Charon, 2008; Frank, 1997; Hydén & Brockmeier, 2008; Spencer, 2020). This kind of attention need not be restricted to clinicians, of course. As evidenced by the evolution of narrative psychology, among other subfields of psychology, there has emerged significant interest on the part of many to adopt a similar approach in their own work, which suggests that movement in the direction of the psychological humanities is already well begun. What would it take for this movement—among other, comparable movements, including those that take us beyond the written word—to more fully realize itself? What might be its rallying cry and most compelling rationales?

One prominent rationale, tied to the earlier discussion of poetic science, is the idea that *poiesis* entails disclosure, revelation, and the "unconcealment" (Heidegger, 1971) of meanings that had theretofore been dormant or inchoate. Through poetry, Jay Parini (2008) has written, "A whole world becomes available to readers that was not there before" (p. 25). Octavio Paz (1967) speaks to this as well in his consideration of the "strangeness" that may emerge when the familiar has been poetically defamiliarized: "Strangeness," he writes, "is wonder at a commonplace reality that is suddenly revealed as that which has never been seen before" (p. 112). Even amidst this never-having-been-seen, there can remain a measure of familiarity and recognition. William James (1982 [1902]) addresses this phenomenon in his discussion of mystical experience. "The simplest rudiment of mystical experience," he writes, "would seem to be that deepened sense of the significance of a maxim or formula which occasionally sweeps over one. 'I've heard that said all my life,' we exclaim, 'but I never realized its full meaning until now'" (p. 382). Such recognition, Gadamer (1986) adds, means "knowing something as that with which we are already acquainted," and it "always implies that we have come to know something more authentically than we were able to do when caught up in our first encounter with it" (p. 47). The situation being described here is a curious, even paradoxical, one. Even amidst the aforementioned process of *de*familiarization, there is a kind of *re*familiarization—that is, a process of seeing anew.

As for why this dual process we are considering is so important, Marilynne Robinson (2012), from whom we heard back in Chapter 1, has some interesting and provocative things to say, when she refers to

> that vivid sense of mine that everything is much more than itself, as commonly reckoned, and that this imaginary island is the haunt of real souls, sacred as they will ever be, though now we hardly know what this means. Paul says we make take the created order as a revelation of God's nature. We now know that there is another reality, beyond the grasp of our comprehension yet wholly immanent in all of Being, powerful in every sense of the word, invisible to our sight, silent to our hearing, foolish to our wisdom, yet somehow steadfast, allowing us our days and years. This is more than metaphor. It is a clear-eyed look at our circumstance.
>
> (p. 224)

And insofar as we can access such circumstance—which is, arguably, one of the central functions and purposes of *poiesis*—we will be that much more likely to find in it a true home.

Given some of what is being said, it may seem that the perspective being advanced is too positive, too wedded to what is good and redemptive and is thus insufficiently cognizant of our profound limitations and vulnerabilities (see especially Fowers et al., 2017). However, making the world "visible" is not restricted to the positive. As Rebecca Solnit has noted in *The Faraway Nearby* (2014),

> Many of the great humanitarian and environmental campaigns of our time have been to make the unknown real, the invisible visible, to bring the faraway near, so that the suffering of sweatshop workers, torture victims, beaten children, even the destruction of other species and remote places, impinges on the imagination and perhaps prompts you to act. It's also a narrative art of explaining the connections between your food or your clothing or your government and this suffering far from sight in which you nonetheless play a role.
>
> (p. 53)

In regard to the suffering that sometimes comes to visit us, "in your own home or bed or life," it "can be harder to see," and so too for "the self who is implicated" (p. 53). Whether faraway or nearby, the challenge and the task remain much the same: to make the unseen seen, the unfelt felt, the unknown known.

"What do writers do when they seriously notice the world?" James Woods asks in *The Nearest Thing to Life* (2015):

> Perhaps they do nothing less than rescue the life of things from their death—from two deaths, one small and one large: from the "death" that literary form always threatens to impose on life, and from actual death. I mean, by the latter, the fading reality that besets details as they recede from us—the memories of our childhood, the almost-forgotten pungency of flavors, smells, textures: the slow death that we deal to the world by the sleep of our attention. By congested habit, or through laziness, lack of curiosity, thin haste, we stop looking at things.
>
> (p. 58)

The task, in short, is "to rescue this adventure from this slow retreat" (p. 59).

At the heart of all of these poetic projects is what Woods (2015), among many others, simply refers to as "noticing": "To notice is to rescue, to redeem, to save life from itself" (p. 63). We might also bring the somewhat more formal term "attention" back into the picture, seeing it as a counterweight, of sorts, to the "ordinary oblivion" that is, arguably, the default condition of our lives (Freeman, 2014a). But of course our task, as psychologists, is not only to attend to the world; as writers—and, in some cases, as artists working in other mediums—it is, as above, to make it seen, felt, and known through the work we do.

As already indicated, one could continue to consider this project a scientific one, essentially in the tradition of the *Geisteswissenschaften* rather than the *Naturwissenschaften*. If that is seen as an important thing to do, given the politics involved in appearing to "jump ship," so be it; the politics are real. Speaking for myself, I am inclined to call the project "post-scientific," which translates roughly as the exploration of that region of experience which remains after science has done its work (Freeman, 2019a). Framed this way, it may seem as if all we will have before us are mere "crumbs," leftovers. But that is not the case at all, for the region being referred to is actually quite large. What's more, following Heidegger, among others, it is primary; it is the very ground of science itself. Here lies the gist of the problem, as I see it: Much of psychological science has eliminated from view some of those very features of human reality that render it human. In doing so, it has thus dehumanized the human, all the while imagining that its objectness is coextensive with its realness. Again, therefore, the problem isn't only that the discipline hasn't been sufficiently pluralistic, in the sense of welcoming new and different approaches to inquiry. It's that much of what we have been left with presents a crude and indeed false image of who and what we are.

As Robinson has suggested in her most recent book, *What Are We Doing Here?* (2018), "It is as if we can only be granted a place in the universe if we are made vastly less extraordinary than we clearly are" (p. 264). And if she is right, psychology is partly to blame:

> The science of the mind, as it is practiced now and as it has been practiced for generations, has no place for human inwardness, the reflective settling into oneself that somehow finds and yields structure and meaning, not all at once but as a kind of unwilled constellating of thoughts and things to which some part of one's attention may have drifted any number of times. It is in the nature of the mind to distill, to do its strange work over time. No snapshots, no series of images, could capture its life.
>
> (p. 265)

"Unless it is to distinguish itself very sharply from theistic tradition," Robinson continues, "I have no idea why the various psychologies are alike in disallowing the more ingratiating human traits" (p. 269). Perhaps one reason is this very divorce.

Sympathetic though I am too much of what Robinson has to say, I have no particular interest in this chapter to tout what is most extraordinary and ingratiating in us. That is part of the story to be told, to be sure, but only a part; it goes without saying that there is much in us that is mean and base too. I don't know that we have done very well with this latter part either. Generally speaking, the image of the human we have been bequeathed is beyond good and evil alike, reduced to those dimensions that render such ethical and moral descriptors all but irrelevant.

This brings us back to the question of theory. "If a theoretical account of the order of things does not describe what reason or intuition propose to the understanding, then the factor that would correct for its deficiencies should be looked to, pondered" (Robinson, 2018, p. 271). This is what I have been trying to do in these pages. If Robinson is right, "We have in ourselves grounds for supposing that Being is vaster, more luminous, more consequential than we have allowed ourselves to imagine for many generations" (p. 271). In the end, I suppose it all comes down to the question of whether she is right. As I have already indicated, Robinson's rendition of things sometimes strikes me as a bit too grand, too taken with our beautiful depths. I am taken with these too, to be sure. But I am also taken aback by other depths, the ones that lead to small-mindedness and hatred and violence. She surely knows these are part of the human picture too, but occasionally her hymns of praise for the miracle that is us feel excessive. (Perhaps the current political climate is making these sorts of claims seem excessive.) Having offered this modest qualification, I find myself fully on board with her resistance to theoreticism—or at least the kind of entrapping theoreticism often seen in psychology. Whether we are as extraordinary as Robinson suggests is a secondary matter. What's primary is the uncontainability of Being itself. It is this, above all else, that calls for a poetics of the Other.

Following Robinson, along with what was said earlier when I discussed some of the implications of Marcuse's (1978) work, the kind of move I am proposing here is particularly urgent within the discipline of psychology as currently constituted. This is because the view of psychology as science that has been promulgated has, wittingly or not, sought to monopolize the discipline, not only on the plane of method and theory but also on the plane of reality itself. It has thus built an edifice based on its own insisted-upon definitions and conceptions of reality. This edifice is a monolith, and even if it has been "softened" to some degree by the emergence of qualitative methods and related pursuits, it remains no less a monolith for all that. Its basic credo: We are to inquire into that which can be objectified, measured, and parsed—that is, into that which seemingly *can* be gotten around; only then, the story goes, will we be building the science so desired. This credo has its place. But it need not, and should not, monopolize the discipline. For, in promoting its own definitions of what is real and mistaking these definitions for reality itself, it has shrunken, violently, the very space of thinking about and exploring the human condition.

I am not proposing to *re*define reality via the poetics of the Other. That would be to substitute one form of monopoly for another. Rather, I am proposing to *de*-define reality, and to do so not in the name of some version of subjectivism but, in a distinct sense, exactly the opposite: By de-defining reality—that is, by stepping back from the kinds of entrapping methodological procedures and theoretical structures most often employed in the discipline—we may be able to move closer to reality itself, the reality that precedes our definitions and categories, the reality that can't be gotten around, the reality that, in its surplus, insists on our recognition of, and reverence for, its irreducible otherness. In view of this perspective, one might plausibly ask: Is this perspective *post*-scientific? Or is it *pre*scientific? For present purposes, I am going to stick with the first of these. It is too late to be prescientific and I have no interest in indulging in nostalgic harking-back, and while I could continue to frame this project as a re-visioning of science, it's not clear what is gained by doing so—except, of course, the kind of currency that science tends to carry in the discipline of psychology. I don't know that we need to serve that master anymore. Less severely: I don't know that we *all* need to serve that master. Let us therefore free ourselves from the tyranny of the monopoly and the claustrophobia of the monolith.

I have no set of discrete guidelines for what we might do instead. Nor do I seek to establish any; it would run counter to the spirit of the project. It is time instead, for some of us at any rate, to think differently about what the discipline is and might be. If there is any limit at all, it is reality itself, holding back, resisting our advances. Beyond that, there is our own imagination, free, within this singular limit, to create entirely new forms of inquiry and expression. These, I suggest, will, of necessity, be poetic in nature and will seek to disclose those features of reality that surpass our entrapping schemes and insist that we be more attentive, respectful, and humble in our efforts to explore the human condition.

In referring to the "poetic," I mean something akin to what poetry does. In a recent (Freeman, 2022b) article simply titled "Poetry," I wrote the following:

> There is no need to offer a formal definition of poetry. It would just be one, there are lots of other definitions that might be brought forth, and there is no reason to try to determine which one(s) to privilege. For present purposes, it is more important to identify what poetry generally *does*, what its functions are and how it enters the world of experience; and what it does, at its core is intimately and necessarily tied to the possible—on at least four, possibly five, levels. The first and most basic level is *semantic*: Poetry employs language, especially metaphorical language, in order to generate new meanings. The second level is *referential*: Poetry can open up and "unconceal" the world, allowing us to see and feel reality in fuller measure. The third level is *musical*: Poetic language is not only about meaning, but sound—the sound of particular words, their rhythm and cadence and melody. The fourth level is *ontological*: In opening up and unconcealing the world, it does much the same for us as readers, allowing us to experience our own interiority and depths. As for the fifth—or the possibility of the fifth—it is *transcendent*: Sometimes, all of the processes just enumerated come together in such a way as to provide an intimation, or even an experience, of the sacred.

A few pages back, I suggested that the "default" condition of the human condition—especially that particular form of it that we have come to find in the contemporary world—may be characterized by "ordinary oblivion," that is, a kind of inattentiveness or "caughtupness" that serves to obscure the world (Freeman, 2014a). Arguably, it has always been this way to some degree; we humans are readily lulled into the comfort of familiarity, routine, "common sense" and sensing. This tendency has been intensified in our time by the great wealth of things that distract us further from beholding what is actually there, before us. Poetry may therefore be more necessary than ever.

Seamus Heaney, in *The Redress of Poetry* (1995), refers to Simone Weil's extraordinary book *Gravity and Grace* (1997 [1952]), which "is informed by the idea of counterweighting, of balancing out the forces, of redress—tilting the scales of reality toward some transcendent equilibrium." So too for the activity of poetry:

> There is a tendency to place a counter-reality in the scales—a reality which may be only imagined but which nevertheless has weight because it is imagined within the gravitational pull of the actual and can therefore hold

> its own and balance out against the historical situation. This redressing effect of poetry comes from its being a glimpsed alternative, a revelation of potential that is denied or constantly threatened by circumstances. And sometimes, of course, it happens that such a revelation, once enshrined in the poem, remains as a standard for the poet, so that he or she must submit to the strain of bearing witness in his or her own life to the plane of consciousness established in the poem.
>
> (pp. 3–4)

As Heaney goes on to suggest, "As long as the coordinates of the imagined thing correspond to those of the world we live in and endure, poetry is fulfilling its counterweighting function. It becomes another truth to which we can have recourse, before which we can know ourselves in a more fully empowered way" (p. 8).

"At its best," Jay Parini (2008) adds, "poetry is a language adequate to our experience" (p. 9) and "restores the culture to itself: mirroring what it finds there already but also sensing and embodying the higher purposes and buried ideals of that culture, granting access to hidden sources of power" (p. 22). Through it, he told us earlier "A whole world becomes available to readers that was not there before" (p. 25)—not, at least, in the same way. In reaching for the poetic, we thus reach for a deeper way, one that is more "adequate to our experience" and, in turn, more adequate to the undisclosed potential the world, inner as well as outer, bears within it.

5 Thinking Otherwise

We can pick up right where we left off in the previous chapter. I almost subtitled that chapter "The Primacy of *Poiesis*." It wouldn't have been entirely unfounded. But it would have been misleading. This is because before *poiesis* there is the *world*, calling it forth. As Mary Oliver tells us, in her book *Upstream* (2016), her biggest sources of inspiration as a writer were the natural world and the world of literature. "And this is what I learned: that the world's *otherness* is antidote to confusion, that standing *within* this otherness—the beauty and mystery of the world, out in the fields or deep inside books—can re-dignify the worst-stung heart" (pp. 14–15). None of this nullified the griefs that would, inevitably, come her way. "But there is, also, the summoning world, the admirable energies of the world, better than anger, better than bitterness and, because more interesting, more alleviating" (p. 20). Oliver's conclusion: "So, it comes first: the world. Then, literature. And then, what one pencil moving over a thousand miles of paper can (perhaps, sometimes) do" (p. 21).

It can be enthralling, indeed. On the occasion of presenting his inaugural address to the College de France (in December 1981), the poet and critic Yves Bonnefoy recollects his initial attraction with the "excess in words" highlighted in surrealist writing:

> What a call, as if from an unknown heaven, in these clusters of lawless tropes! What energy, it seemed, in this unpredictable bubbling up from the depths of language! But once the initial fascination was over, I took no joy in these words which I was told were free. I had before my eyes another kind of evidence, nourished by other poets, the evidence of running water, of a fire burning peacefully in our daily existence, and of time and chance of which these realities are made, and it seemed to me fairly soon that the transgressions of automatic writing were less the desired surreality, existing beyond the too superficial realisms of controlled thought whose signifieds remain fixed, than a reluctance to raise the question of the self, whose richest potentiality is perhaps in the life that one takes on day after day, without illusions, in the midst of what is simple. What are all the

DOI: 10.4324/9780429323652-6

> subtleties of language, after all, even turned upside down in a thousand different ways, next to the perception one can have, directly, mysteriously, of the movement of the leaves against the sky, or of the noise fruit makes when it falls into the grass? And always throughout this whole time I kept in mind, as an encouragement and even as a proof, the moment when the young reader opens passionately a great book and finds words, of course, but also things and people, and the horizon, and the sky: in short, a whole world given all at once to his thirst.
>
> (1989, p. 162)

Notice what is being said here: Somehow the world—the movement of leaves and the noise of falling fruit—can find its way into words, such that another world emerges. And "this world which cuts itself off from the world seems to the person who creates it not only more satisfying than the first but also more real." The consequence is that we, as readers, may experience the "impression of a reality at last fully incarnate" (p. 164). Something has been real-ized, made real, and in this making, the world may be refound.

In a related vein, Robinson (2018) cites a quote from the composer Robert Schumann that goes roughly as follows: "To compose music one need only remember a song no one has ever heard before." Robinson herself goes on to speak of "the sense of answering to what is unconsciously and intimately known, perhaps known more deeply because it is still very widely potential, the song we could not know we yearned to hear" (pp. 110–111). What a strange idea! "Does art call up a response that is essentially the recognition of a new thing?" (p. 111). I suppose we can set aside this brainteaser. One thing seems clear in any case: "Experience demands a richer vocabulary than theory can give it" (p. 112). It also demands unwavering attention to and respect for what is *other*, both human and nonhuman. This is what is primary; this is what has priority. And in the face of it, in its inexhaustible abundance, one must turn to the poetic, broadly conceived.

Why "must" one do so, though? Were I to have simply issued a call to the poetic—as in, "Here's another way of going about exploring things"—there wouldn't be much to contest. But my claim is a stronger one, the call in question being nothing short of a necessity. As we have already seen, the reason it is a necessity is that the living presence of the reality we call "human" actively resists the kind of empirical and theoretical enclosure characteristic of science, especially natural science. This, again, is not necessarily a fault of science. Science is, arguably, predicated upon such enclosure, and we ought not to fault it for what it is patently unprepared to do, at least in its current, dominant form. And it is patently unprepared to address the living presence of human reality—as well as certain features of nonhuman reality.

Jean-Luc Marion's (2008) notion of "the saturated phenomenon" is particularly relevant here. The saturated phenomenon is that which "refuses to let itself be looked at as an object, precisely because it appears with a multiple and indescribable excess that suspends any effort at constitution." However, this doesn't mean that it cannot be addressed and explored. "To define the saturated phenomenon as a nonobjective or, more exactly, nonobjectivizable phenomenon in no way indicates a refuge in the irrational or the arbitrary." On the contrary, "this definition refers to one of its distinctive properties: although exemplarily visible, it nevertheless cannot be looked at"—if, by "looked," we mean "under the control of the one who is seeing" (p. 43). The constituting *I* is thus displaced from this perspective, dethroned. Indeed, "Far from being able to constitute this phenomenon, the *I* experiences itself as constituted by it." This is "because it no longer has at its disposal any dominant point of view over the intuition that overwhelms it." As such, "it becomes a *me* rather than an *I*" (p. 44). As Marion goes on to note, we ought not to consider the saturated phenomenon a "limit case, an exceptional, vaguely irrational, in short, a 'mystical' case of phenomenality" (p. 45). Rather, we find the saturated phenomenon whenever we encounter those phenomena that, by virtue of what they patently *are*, resist the dominating efforts of the imperial I. "(W)hen and why must one resort to the hypothesis of the saturated phenomenon?" The answer is basic enough: "One must do so each time one admits that it is impossible to subsume an intuition in an adequate concept . . . —in other words, each time one must renounce thinking a phenomenon as an object if one wants to think it as it shows itself" (p. 127). The flesh and blood human, standing before me, visible yet utterly unassimilable to my grasp, my comprehension, would appear to be a notable one.

Thus far, it has been suggested that human reality, understood as presence or phenomenon rather than object, eludes the kind of empirical and theoretical containment science generally seeks. We had no reason to fault science for this; it is what it is. We can, however, fault science—or at least some of those who aspire to be scientists—to the degree that it seeks to colonize that which would appear to be "out of bounds," as it were, owing to the unobjectivizable phenomenality of its presence. Heidegger's (1977) language of entrapment is thus particularly, and problematically, apt in this context. In much of contemporary psychology, the human animal, wild and unruly in its way, is caged and domesticated, subjected to this experiment or that inventory, all in the hope that the resultant data will allow us to piece back together a portrait of who and what we might be. Unfortunately, it is, inevitably, too late.

It's not just that human reality, as living presence, eludes such entrapment. Following Levinas (1999), especially, it's that certain features of human reality—most notably, the face of the Other—hold us in thrall: "there arises, awakened before the face of the other, a responsibility for the other to whom I was committed before any committing, *before* being present to myself or coming back to self" (1999, pp. 30–31). This responsibility, therefore, "is not reducible to a thought going back to an idea given in the past to the 'I think' and rediscovered by it" (p. 32). Rather, it issues *from the Other*. Levinas goes on in this text to address the problem of representation, not only in the context of the beholding of the Other, but in other contexts as well, and is particularly interested in questioning "the exclusive privilege that Western culture has conferred on consciousness" (p. 125). On this account, there is "a meaningfulness prior to representation, in which transcendental philosophy situated the origin of thought" (p. 130), and this meaningfulness, immanent in the face of the Other, among other phenomena, calls for something *other* than science-style theorization. Indeed, and again, if we are to speak of theory at all, it is that form of it which *precedes* such theorization and which entails a kind of mindful beholding of, and surrender to, the Other.

As Levinas (1985) has stated elsewhere, echoing some of the ideas advanced by Marion (and, as we saw back in Chapter 1, by Marcel), "Knowledge has always been interpreted as assimilation. Even the most surprising discoveries end by being absorbed, comprehended, with all that there is of 'prehending' in 'comprehending'." The problem, however, is that "the most audacious and remote knowledge does not put us in communion with the truly other; it does not take the place of sociality; it is still and always a solitude" (p. 60)—that is, an act of the putatively sovereign *I*, having its way, one might say, with the objectifiable world. To sum up:

> The statement that others do not appear to me as objects does not just mean that I do not take the other person as a thing under my power, a "something." It also asserts that the very relation originally established between myself and others, between myself and someone, cannot properly be said to reside in an act of knowledge that, as such, is seizure and comprehension, the besiegement of objects.
>
> (Levinas, 1994, p. 40)

As Levinas (1996) adds, "Concrete reality is man"—and others-than-man—"always already in relation to the world. . . . These relations cannot be reduced to theoretical representation. The latter would only confirm the autonomy of the thinking subject, . . . the subject closed in on itself" (p. 19). Moreover, these relations cannot be seen exclusively in cognitive terms. For what Levinas is talking about here is the flesh and blood human being, demanding us, calling us beyond ourselves (see also Goodman, 2012). For Levinas, in short, it is imperative that we think Otherwise about these matters. I heartily concur (Freeman, 2012, 2014a). Also imperative is that we, theoretical and philosophical psychologists, especially, carry out work that is in keeping with such thinking in a portion of what we do. This work is what I have herein been calling a "poetics," and it is nothing more, and nothing less, than the language required in the face of the Other's ungraspable, unobjectivizable, and untheorizable priority. (My apologies for all the big words.) I will explore this set of issues in greater depth and detail later on, in Chapter 6, focusing explicitly on the ethical dimension of the kind of encounter Levinas is addressing.

Important though attentiveness to the flesh and blood other person is, the idea of the Other ought not to be restricted to the human alone but can profitably be extended to those "nonhuman regions of 'otherness'" Mary Oliver (2016) talked about, especially nature, as well as aesthetic experience, religious experience, and other such sites. These, in their own distinctive ways, are as uncontainable as the concrete reality of the human and they too "require different modes of thinking and writing"—and, perhaps, different modes of theorizing—"than those ordinarily associated with theoretical reflection" (Freeman, 2000, p. 76). The Other, again, therefore, refers to nothing less than the *world*, both human and nonhuman, lying beyond the perimeter of the self.

For Oliver, you may recall, it isn't only the natural world that serves as inspiration but the world of literature as well. Let me take as an example some of the work I have done on my mother, who died at age 93 after a dozen or so years of being afflicted with dementia (Freeman, 2021b). As (something of) a psychologist, I am not interested in merely "telling her story" in the manner of a (loving) biographer-son. As a longtime student of memory, identity, and related issues, I want to do more; I want to speak to these issues in a meaningful way, maybe even in a way that will contribute to "knowledge" about dementia, memory, identity, and so on. I need to proceed carefully and cautiously as I go about this work. I am only considering a single "case," the case happens to be my mother, and I am hardly in the position of being able to universalize, or even generalize robustly, about the "findings" at hand. They are *not* findings—certainly not in the customary sense of the word. They are not a function of discrete methodological procedures, they do not and cannot stand apart from the story I seek to tell, and it is patently clear that what I saw transpire through the course of my mother's—and my—life over the course of those dozen years is unique to *us*. This doesn't mean that there are no bridges to be built between our situation and those of others; there can be and there are. I therefore hope that others facing similar circumstances will read and benefit from the work I do, seeing in this particular case dimensions of experience and meaning they can relate to their own situations. I also hope that researchers and scholars in psychology and beyond—gerontology, dementia studies, and narrative studies among them—will read and benefit from this work, seeing it not only as a (good, I hope) story but a piece of psychological scholarship able to make some modest contribution to the relevant fields.

At the same time, it is absolutely essential that this work, or at least significant portions of it, be "literary" in nature as well. In the particular form of narrative knowing and narrative writing I practice, there is not only no detaching the findings from the story I seek to tell but there is also no detaching the content of what I say from the sensuous and sonorous materiality of the words I use to say it. The medium in question, therefore—language—is not merely a vehicle for transmitting information; it *matters* in a way that scientific writing generally does not. What's more, it seeks to carry not only the cognitive dimension of what is being said but also *feeling*; it seeks to express, evoke, and may, at times, even *move*. I don't *seek* to move readers, mind you, certainly not in any calculated way. Rather, I need to find words that can somehow carry the emotional weight of the phenomena and bring it forth so that readers can feel it too, in their own distinctive ways.

There is another feature of this sort of work to be emphasized as well, one that brings us closer still to the terrain of the arts and humanities. Not unlike human beings themselves, work of the sort being described, and, following Gadamer (1986), literary work more generally, tends to resist pure conceptualization and theorization, and often brings forth a resonance, a non-thematizable presence, that exceeds grasp and comprehension. I don't want to take this line of argument too far; I wouldn't want to place narrative knowing and writing too far from the aim of "understanding." But if literary work seeks to "understand," it does so in a different way than science tends to do. Indeed, one might plausibly say that, in many works of literature—as well as in hybrid forms of the sort I have just described—empathy, sympathy, and compassion take precedence; understanding may occur in their wake, when one seeks to take stock of what has been said and felt and draws out the relevant implications, but it is, in a sense, secondary to the literary "effects" that emerge in and through the process of reading. Notice here the connection to what Levinas said about encountering the human Other: Before there is understanding, there is the concrete reality of the Other, drawing me out of myself.

As an important side note, some of what I discussed in the previous paragraph concerning the potential value of the work I (and others) do for generating knowledge pertinent to psychology marks a point of distinction between "pure" literature and art and artful psychology, situated as part of the psychological humanities: If the former seek generally to leave conclusions and "takeaways" to the audience (readers, viewers, and listeners), the latter generally seek to say something of a more declarative sort about the phenomenon or phenomena being explored. In this respect, there is *some* measure of detachability of what is being said from the manner of its saying, but of a limited sort, one that gestures in some direction pertinent to the phenomenon or phenomena in question but, of necessity, stops short of those more robust conclusions and takeaways that are the norm in most psychological inquiry.

As Karl Ove Knausgaard (2018) has written, in a little book called *Inadvertent*, "Art and literature constitute a continual negotiation with reality, they represent an exchange between identity and culture and the material, physical, and endlessly complex world they arise from" (p. 11). By virtue of this negotiation, "literature by its very nature always seeks complexity and ambiguity." It therefore seeks to indict and redress "monologic claims of truth about the world" (p. 11), especially as these are advanced as "common sense" about the way things are. Indeed, "writing," Knausgaard writes, "is precisely about disregarding how something seems in the eyes of others, it is precisely about freeing oneself from all kinds of judgments and from posturing and positioning. Writing is about making something accessible, allowing something to reveal itself" (p. 27). It is also about disregarding, or trying to disregard, one's own potentially calcified preconceptions and controlling designs, thereby allowing what is *other* to speak. Knausgaard's goal: "to erode my own notions about the world, allowing whatever had been kept down by them to rise to the surface." There is only one way to achieve this, he insists: "to abdicate as king of myself and let the literary, in other words writing and the forms of writing, lead the way" (pp. 38–39).

Following both Oliver and Knausgaard, attention to what is other is key. Literature, among the other arts, is a prime vehicle for not only sharpening this attention but also preserving and sustaining it. It is, as the title of James Woods's most recent (2015) book suggests, "the nearest thing to life," its foremost aim, as he told us earlier, "to rescue this adventure from this slow retreat" (p. 59). The same may be said of the other arts as well.

As already noted, I call this slow retreat about which Woods speaks "ordinary oblivion," and I consider it the default mode of being human. Deep though our capacities for noticing the world may be, they tend to "retreat" and become diminished; the centrifugal energies that issue from what is other thus get swallowed up by the centripetal energies of the ego-driven, preoccupied, inattentive self. Certain things may awaken us from this oblivion—love, perhaps, or tragedy, or even just a beautiful day, enjoining us to notice and to wonder. But the attention we are considering is a fragile one. How soon we retreat. How soon we *forget*. Literature and the arts, in their "rescue" function, thus emerge as mnemonic devices, as it were, devices for noticing and remembering, perhaps loving.

Much of what goes on in contemporary psychology is, arguably, an accomplice to our oblivion and amnesia. This is especially so in how it tends to address persons. They, we, are often hidden from view by their neurotransmitters or their personality traits or the vast array of variables so often adduced in the hope of gaining some measure of certainty about life. That's fine; there is no need to shut the door on the standard fare. There is, however, a profound and urgent need to open the door to other approaches, other modes of knowing, ones that bring us nearer to persons themselves, nearer to life. These new ways are part of the terrain of the arts and humanities.

I do not wish to overstate the distinction, or the gulf, between the psychological sciences and the psychological humanities. There are works of science that bear within them a deep humanity. Likewise, there are works of literature that, in their aim of bringing us nearer to life, bear within them a deep scientificity, in the sense of practicing fidelity to the proverbial "things themselves." Indeed, and again, one might plausibly say that there is a kind of objectivity in such works—not in the customary sense of methodological detachment, the insistence on precise measures, and all the rest but in the aforementioned sense of an attentive, respectful care for the phenomena, in all of their ambiguity, messiness, and possible beauty. It is a more primordial form of objectivity, one that seeks to "[allow] something to reveal itself," as Knausgaard had put it, something heretofore unarticulated, inchoate. So it is that we sometimes find in works of art and literature what Bonnefoy (1989) had referred to as the "impression of a reality at last fully incarnate" (p. 164), fully realized and made known. That is not all. What we may also find in such works is a kind of resonant particularity—which is to say, a form of particularity that somehow moves beyond itself and speaks to some larger sphere. In this respect, there is a generalizing, or even universalizing, function "built-in" to these works, woven into their very fabric.

Can works of psychology actually *become* works of literature and art? Can they generate the incarnational resonance just considered and thereby bring us nearer to life? I believe they can. They will be works of a unique sort—hybrid forms, as I called them earlier, that hover in the space between science and art, perhaps serving to diminish the distance between the two. By clearing an adequate space for them, through the psychological humanities, psychology may finally succeed in becoming more adequate to the human condition and thereby further realizing itself as a discipline.

6 Fidelity to Other Persons

In the previous chapter, I spoke briefly about some of the work I have done about my mother (Freeman, 2021b; see also 2008a, 2008b)—which, I should avow, is also about both me and our relationship. In that context, I mainly addressed the kind of work I aspired to create, the kind of impact I hoped it would have, and how it might be seen as a contribution to the psychological humanities. In this chapter, I want to explore some of the interpretive challenges entailed in carrying out the work and, eventually, telling her story. I also want to dig deeper into the ethical dimension of encountering the Other, focusing especially on the demand my mother made on me as a person in need. Finally, I want to say more about the work itself, which, in many respects, embodies the kind of work that might be considered part of the psychological humanities.

I do want to note once more that the vision of the psychological humanities I have been putting forth thus far in these pages is but one variant of what might be included under its umbrella. For Thomas Teo (2017), for instance, the aim, or at least one of the aims, is to build a general theory of subjectivity, drawing on disciplines including philosophy, history, political and social theories, as well as indigenous, cultural, and postcolonial theories. For Sugarman and Martin (2020b), the focus is more on personhood. "In the contemporary academy," they write,

> the humanities include, but are not exhausted by, literature and linguistics, history and historiography, musicology, theatre, art, media, religious and cultural studies, and the philosophical and theoretical study of these and related disciplines and undertakings. Central to the humanities, however historicized and classified, are concerns about humans as particular kinds of beings, their contexts, their activities, and their experiences.
>
> (p. 1).

For their purposes, nowhere is the turn to the humanities more necessary, and urgent, than in studying and understanding human persons. This is because

> the person is much more than a physical, biological being. To be a person requires being immersed in social and cultural practices that constitute

DOI: 10.4324/9780429323652-7

> ways and traditions of life, replete with values that guide our decisions and actions, perspectives, and possibilities for acting in consort with others, narratives that shape our existence, and strategies and designs for undertaking life projects. All of this is the very stuff of humanities disciplines like literary and cultural studies, history, anthropology, philosophy, languages, political studies, and the arts.
>
> (pp. 1–2)

Other variants of the psychological humanities have emerged (e.g., Slaney, 2020), and are continuing to emerge. All of this is by way of reiterating that the specific set of concerns found herein are a function of my own intellectual interests and predilections and my own, inevitably idiosyncratic, way into the project.

Returning to my work about my mother, one very basic interpretive challenge has to do with the fact that, when her situation became severe, I couldn't possibly fathom what was going on in her mind; it was far too distant and alien. Moreover, she eventually arrived at a point at which she was all but storyless: Due to the deterioration of her memory, she came to live her life largely beyond narrative, her experiential world being confined mainly to the moment. But even before this level of deterioration and impairment, there was a vast gulf between much of what she would say and what I took her words to mean. Early on, for instance, my mother would often protest mightily, against both the situation in which she had found herself and those of us entrusted with her care. Whether it was her ability to drive, write a check, or simply remember what she had said only seconds before, she would strike out in anger, finding it inconceivable that anything had changed. So it was that I (2008a) would eventually write that some of what she said could be seen as the "product of a culture that, in a distinct sense, refuses to admit the reality of decline, and death, into its midst." I also referred to the existence of a "dual narrative . . . operating behind the scenes of consciousness." First, there was "the narrative of the vital, self-sufficient Individual, who resists the kind of fragility, vulnerability, and dependency that growing old sometimes brings in tow" (p. 176). Second, there was "the narrative of inexorable decline," which, in a distinct sense, operates in tandem with—and is on some level parasitic upon—the first. Basically, then, my mother's words and demeanor suggested to me some of the ways in which certain aspects of culturally rooted features of subjectivity—having to do with autonomy, self-sufficiency, the denial of death, and more—had become inscribed in her being. In a section of this piece called "Deconstructing the cultural story," I expressed the wish that she could let some of her frustration and anger go. I even offered some counter-narratives—for instance, about vulnerability and dependency and fragility, and how these were okay. Unfortunately, they never quite took; she was in too deep. In any case, were I to have presented some of my interpretations to her at this phase, she would have found most of them incomprehensible or irrelevant, for in her mind, she was still "just fine."

Later on, there would be other, equally difficult situations. One day, when I stopped by her apartment, for instance, she had the telephone directory open to the page that included her name and number. At the top of the page, she had scrawled her name. The ink was heavy and dark, the "F" circled, and in the column of names, hers was underlined, roughly and repeatedly. I will not pretend to know exactly what was going through her mind at the time, but there can be little doubt that she was trying to find what seemed to be irretrievably lost. Later still, she would sometimes have no idea where—or who—she was. This might happen upon her waking from a nap and finding everything around her unfamiliar and strange. It's hard to imagine what her world must have been like. As she said to me one time, it wasn't like being in a new place. Rather, it was like being in "another world" (Freeman, 2021b, p. 73).

I needn't say more here about the interpretive challenges I faced in trying to make sense of her experience. Suffice it to say that they were large and significant and that they forced me to stretch and expand my own interpretive categories. These could only go so far, though, for her words, her gestures, her way of being, and her *life* exceeded what I could ever truly know.

This brings me more directly to the ethical dimension of the situation. I didn't intend to write about my mother. More than anything, I approached my mother as a son, not a "researcher" or writer. But as a student of narrative interested in exploring issues of memory and identity in the context of people's lives, I wasn't one to ignore what I was seeing. Indeed, painful though aspects of those years were, I confess to having been fascinated, at times, too. The fact is I was learning things about memory and identity, in her life, in mine, and in our relationship, that I could never have learned otherwise. We also *felt* things we would never have felt. There were times, in fact, when it seemed as if entirely new regions of being had been opened up owing to the very intimacy of our evolving relationship. I know some people were taken aback by my decision to write about all of this, but for me, it didn't feel like a decision at all. I had to do it.

It wasn't easy (see especially Freeman, 2019b, 2021b). One very basic reason, again, is that I was (am?) her son, so as one of my good friends commented, it was hard to imagine how I could "distance" myself enough from the situation at hand to transform it into an object of inquiry. This person, in fact, had referred to the unusual capacity I had to "objectify" what was going on in my life. I sensed both admirations in her words—for my ability to build a bridge between my life and my work, as well as repulsion—for what may have seemed like a voyeuristic venture out of bounds. She was much more the dispassionate empirical researcher than I was, so that was part of it, but the sheer fact that I was exploring and writing about my *mother* was what made her most uncomfortable. I am sure she wasn't alone in this. In fact, I know she wasn't. This is because I myself was sometimes uncomfortable doing what I was doing. At some point during the early years of my mother's dementia, I would hear her say something that I found poignant or profound, and I would take out my cell phone and type it out. Should I be doing that? Should I really be taking a brief time-out from being her son so I could preserve her, and sometimes my, words? And should I eventually try to take all of these "data" and form them into stories, for conferences and journal articles and books like this one?

Also challenging was the fact that my mother couldn't really consent to what I was doing—not, at least, in the informed consent mode of most social science. I did tell her that I was writing about her, and in true mother (or at least *my* mother) fashion, she seemed delighted by it. "Ma," I might say, "as you know, I've been thinking and writing about people's lives for a long time, focusing on topics like memory and self. And some of what you're experiencing now is actually pretty relevant. Is it okay if I share some things about you and your experience in my writing?" "Of course you can write about me!" she would say. My son, the professor, the writer. She was positively *verklempt*.

But she had only the most minimal idea of what I would write about. In fact, she had only the most minimal idea she had fallen victim to dementia. The day she was diagnosed (with Alzheimer's, actually) she sobbed. Yet that very night, she had no memory at all of having been diagnosed or having been to a doctor. She knew during the early years that things were amiss; she sometimes spoke of being "like a child" or being "brainless." She also knew during the early years that the assisted living residence that she had moved to wasn't just for "senior living," but for those who, in some way or other, were in significant physical or mental need. Remarkably enough, however, she reached a point fairly quickly in which she had virtually no knowledge at all that she was afflicted with dementia. Does it matter that she would become the subject of my musings with nary a clue of what the substance of these musings was? And, now that she is gone, does it matter that she became the focus of a book about the final years of her life? There have been times through the years when I felt that I was somehow taking advantage of her situation, "using" her. This is surely so on some level. What justifies it? *Anything?* I don't have a clean answer to this question, and I'm not sure that I need one.

Having avowed this aspect of the ethical challenge, I never approached my mother as a researcher—or at least I don't think I did. I never arrived at her place with any research agenda. I never had any specific questions in mind. Nor did I ever hope to "get" anything from her; whatever I "got," by way of profound words, meaningful actions, and so on, had emerged in the course of our relationship, through the many hours each week that I spent with her. In what follows, therefore, I won't be addressing how the research relationship evolved but will instead focus on our interpersonal relationship: how it moved, by degrees, from being one in which I had my own *personal* agenda—my own images of how she ought to be responding to her situation, my own attempts to direct the course of things, my own "corrections" of her "misguided" view of her life, and so on—to one in which *she* became the true priority and I, in turn, her "hostage" (Levinas, 1996).

This idea of being a hostage may seem odd, even unrelated, but it came to be an important idea in Levinas's thinking. What does he mean by it, and how might it apply in the present context? In his essay "Substitution" (1996), Levinas spends some time addressing the curious state of the ego: "The ego is not merely a being endowed with certain so-called moral qualities, qualities which it would bear as attributes," but instead is always in the process "of being emptied of its being, of being turned inside out." Moreover, "The ego is not a being which is capable of expiating for others; it is this original expiation which is involuntary because prior to the initiative of the will" (p. 86). In keeping with Levinas's idea of responsibility as being beyond thematization, beyond some principle that I might apply to this or that situation, we see here its involuntary nature. And it is precisely this involuntary dimension—our "captivation," one might say, by the Other—that leads him to the metaphor of the hostage: "It is through the condition of being a hostage that there can be pity, compassion, pardon, and proximity in the world—even the little there is, even the simple 'after you sir'" (p. 91). Or, in the case of my relationship with my mother, even the simple "Hey, ma. Want to go outside and sit in the sun for a while, feel the warm breeze, maybe have a sweet snack?" I will do whatever you want, whatever you need. Period.

If truth be told, it would take some time before I could give myself over to my mother in this way. Even then, this giving-over was, and could only be, partial—aspirational, one might say—owing to the ostensibly inevitable intrusion of my own ego-driven needs and wishes, issuing their own demands. Indeed, it may be that being there for the other is never wholly unalloyed, ego-free, and "pure." For, however primordial the ethical relation may be, it can be and frequently is overwhelmed by what Iris Murdoch (1970), following Freud in broad outline, has referred to as the "fat relentless ego" (p. 51). This is no doubt one reason why human relations are as fraught as they are.

Not only did it take time to give myself over to my mother, it took time before I could let her be who she was. I wasn't alone in this.

> "She was so beautiful, my sister," her elder sister Shirley would say. "I can't bear to see her like this." Another of her sisters basically concluded that my mother was gone. "She left us a long time ago," she said. I don't want to fault them for their feelings. And visually, using the standard "aging gracefully" indicators, my mother was a far cry from what she'd been: She had missing teeth, her face looked hollowed out, her skin was all black and blue, she was confined to a wheelchair, unable to move on her own, often kind of zoned out. By all indications, she was barely there. And, of course, there was the decimation of her memory, or at least of those aspects that visitors from afar so wanted to see, to recognize. All but gone. They so wanted her to be what she had been before. And she wasn't. She had become something scarily *other*, and for some, it was a terrible shock to the system.
>
> (Freeman, 2021b, p. 111)

As I went on to state, there were times when I too "just wanted her to be other than who she'd become; I too wanted her to be the smart, vibrant, attractive woman she had once been. We all wanted to freeze her in time—which is to say, we refused to let her own decay and death enter our lives" (p. 112), and by virtue of this, we could not truly *see* her in her otherness, her difference, her unique integrity as a person.

Some of Martin Buber's (1965) words come to mind in this context:

> This person is other, essentially other than myself, and this otherness of his is what I mean, because I mean him; I confirm it; I wish his otherness to exist, because I wish his particular being to exist. . . . That the men with whom I am bound up in the body politic and with whom I have directly or indirectly to do, are essentially other than myself, that this one or that one does not have merely a different mind, or way of thinking or feeling, or a different conviction or attitude, but has also a different perception of the world, a different recognition and order of meaning, a different touch from the regions of existence, a different faith, a different soil: to affirm all this, to affirm it in the way of a creature, in the midst of the hard situations of conflict, without relaxing their real seriousness, is the way by which we may officiate as helpers in this wide realm entrusted to us as well, and from which alone we are from time to time permitted to touch in our doubts, in humility and upright investigation, on the other's "truth" or "untruth," "justice" or "injustice."
>
> (pp. 61–62)

On Buber's account, we must somehow deepen our attention to and regard for others as the irreducibly unique, and worthy, beings they are. We must in fact "affirm all this," take it to heart. We must care for them too.

The more I was able to see my mother for who she was, the easier it was to care for her. From a Levinasian point of view, this stands to reason: Once I was able to behold her in her otherness and unique integrity, I was immediately held hostage, drawn forth by her, in responsibility and care. I very much like how Iris Murdoch (1970) puts the matter when she suggests that "true vision occasions right conduct." As she admits, "This could be uttered simply as an enlightening tautology," but in her view it can in fact be confirmed by experience itself, which suggests that, "The more the separateness and differentness of other people is realized, and the fact that another man has needs and wishes as demanding as one's own, the harder it becomes to treat a person as a thing" (p. 64). Indeed.

As I have noted elsewhere (Freeman, 2014a), I have no interest in portraying myself as some sort of caregiver-hero. There were times when I thought about going over to see her and didn't. In addition, and again, there were times when my own preoccupations took center stage, with the result that she became veiled, her face all but occluded from view. I also avow that there were some quite mundane, even ego-centric, reasons for my going to see her. As I had (2014a) put the matter, "I go to see her because that's what you're supposed to do, or so she knows what a good son I am, or to assuage some of my own guilt. But," I continued,

> I also go to see her for *her*—because she is alone and in need and my visit brings her one of her few moments of pleasure in life. It's not easy. I often dread going up in the elevator to her floor; there is always something disturbing or depressing going on. Leaving is no better. I go marching off to work or dinner while she sits in a circle with fading, withered, like-minded others, watching some awful TV show or tapping a balloon into the air during "recreation" period. But in the middle is . . . *her*, her simple presence, disrupting me, drawing me forward, outward. She is sitting in a wheelchair, slouched, eyes closed. I walk over and tap her lightly on her shoulder or fiddle playfully with her hair. Her eyes crawl open, she turns her head toward me, and she smiles a faint but radiant smile. I so want her to feel whatever joy she can.
>
> (p. 20)

In the end, I came to see the relationship I established with my mother, and the more general aim of approaching another person emptied of self-interest and giving oneself over to her in care, as a kind of ideal type—which is to say, a form of human relatedness that bears within it just the kind of being-held-hostage by the Other that Levinas has described. He has been criticized for being hyperbolic in framing human relatedness in this way. Insofar as I have followed his lead in broad outline, I may be open to a similar criticism. Hostage language aside, the demand here is to try to meet others where they are, no matter where they are, and to do so without judgment, expectations, needs, and wishes—without *will*, in a way. It may ultimately be impossible. But holding such an attitude in mind, as a kind of regulative idea and ideal, may nevertheless be of value in carrying out our work—as well as living out the kind of human relations to which we might aspire.

This brings us back to Oliver (2016), Knausgaard (2018), and the many others who, in one way or another, insist that, before there is literature and art, there is, as Oliver put it, "the summoning world," demanding our attention and care. In a sense, she is implying that there is, and can be, no literature or art worthy of the name unless there is such attention. Murdoch (1970) would seem to concur: "(T)he greatest art is 'impersonal' because it shows us the world, our world and not another one, with a clarity which startles and delights us simply because we are not used to looking at the real world at all" (p. 63). Moreover, "great art teaches us how real things can be looked at and loved without being seized and used, without being appropriated into the greedy organism of the self" (p. 65). I am not saying that what I have written about my mother is to be considered great art! All I am saying is that attention to what is other may be seen as a precondition for creating something worthy—that is, something that can "show us the world" and thereby draw us out of our potential oblivion and blindness. I could have written about my mother before the transformation I have been discussing. But the resultant work couldn't possibly have possessed the kind of resonance some of it came to possess.

Does the book I wrote deserve to be called "literature" or "art"? I don't know—or care. But it certainly deserves to be considered an entry into the psychological humanities, at least as I envision it. Indeed, some of what I say toward the end of the book may be seen as virtually definitive of my own approach. Let me enumerate some criteria and paraphrase some of what I wrote there.

First and foremost, I have tried to tell the story in its full measure—that is, in all of its dimensions, from the tragic and horrifying all the way to the comic and redemptive. Needless to say by now (I hope), I am speaking here not of offering some sort of definitive, exhaustive account, but one that speaks to the full range of my mother's, and my, experience. In the present context, this meant practicing fidelity to the realities before me, which in turn meant moving beyond the somewhat more unidimensional categories of "tragedy," "comedy," and so on, and preserving what I could of the tensions and tonalities at hand through writing.

Second, I tried to tell this story in a way that was truly attentive to, and respectful of, my mother herself, *her* personhood and *her* world. This doesn't mean that I left myself out of the picture; I couldn't even if I had wanted to. But one of the things I learned through the years is how important it was to bracket my view of things and to see, and respect, hers. I might have wished that she were more cognizant of how much my family and I cared for her during the early years when she protested her condition and felt infantilized and abandoned. I *did* wish this. I also might have wished that she could see better, or that she were more active, or that she cared when I wasn't there. I might have wished, in other words, that she was the same as she had been, before dementia came her way. But she wasn't. So, it became important not only to see her for who she had become but to find the words to speak to it. Her existence, of course, exceeded whatever I might have wished to say about it; it was that which was not to be gotten around; it was a saturated phenomenon; and it was a demand, of the sort not to be encapsulated or thematized or "explained," in some quasi-scientific way. The challenge was thus a poetic one, and I can only hope that readers can find a *person* in the book, in all of her unfathomable, bountiful being.

Third, even as I sought to tell this story in a way that acknowledges and respects difference, otherness, and so on, I also sought to tell it in a way that underscores the essential humanness and dignity of the person. My mother was not an alien being; she was a *human* being, who, even amidst her myriad maladies, infirmities, and occasional oddities, displayed wonderfully human traits: humor, wit, compassion, care, love. I tried to keep these qualities visible. I also tried to keep visible her personhood itself. As I learned firsthand, even when the autobiographical self has all but left the scene, the person, with her unique character and way of being in the world, may remain. It was important that readers see this, precisely for the sake of *humanizing* a category of persons for whom dehumanization often seems like the default.

Fourth, and perhaps most important in the present context, I tried to tell this story in a way that allowed my mother to "live on the page," and to thereby have the kind of expressive, evocative presence that we more often find in works of literature than psychology. I am not referring here to embellishment or ornamentation, to somehow "dressing up" the story in an overtly literary way. I'm speaking instead, again, of the profound challenge of finding language that can serve to open up the reality and the truth of the lives being explored. Ultimately, this may be the deepest and most fundamental rationale for more visibly including the psychological humanities within the discipline of psychology. The fact is, if one wants to speak the language of human experience and do so in a way that does justice to it and reveals its uncontainable intricacies and undisclosed potentialities, doing so is nothing short of a necessity.

7 Fidelity to the Otherness Within

This principle, or "urging," is likely to be seen by some readers as more loaded than the ones discussed thus far. Insofar as the discipline of psychology remains committed mainly to the research mode, its attention remains largely outward-oriented, toward other people. Plus, of course, for all that psychology has sought throughout its history to find a place for internal experience and selfhood, it has been notoriously difficult to find one with any staying power. Not unlike what was said earlier, the project has been deemed too subjective and unwieldy. Indeed, some psychologists—the behaviorists, most notably—saw the project as thoroughly misconceived and thus doomed from the start. As for the attempts that have been made, in fields like personality and social psychology, they have generally marshalled first-person "data" in the service of third-person scientific accounts. A good example of this strategy can be found in the work of Dan McAdams and his colleagues (McAdams, 2006; McAdams & Pals, 2006), who have generated important research and theory showing how "narrative identity" (McAdams & McLean, 2013) plays a pivotal role in the formation of personality. There is also the vast volume of work carried out on self-esteem, self-concept, self-efficacy, and so on. Some of this work is good and valuable, especially if the goal is to build a science of personality or self or identity. But this very approach is a far cry from the kind of self-oriented psychology that James (1950 [1890], 1982 [1902]) wrote about and a far cry from the kind of hermeneutically oriented psychology being considered herein.

I am not, of course, suggesting that all psychology become first-person psychology; that would be imperialistic and wrongheaded. Nor I am suggesting that it ought to be autobiographical or "autoethnographic" (Bochner, 2001; Bochner & Ellis, 2016; Ellis, 2009). Personally speaking, I support this sort of work, have done some of it myself (Freeman, 2002b, 2021b), and would very much like to see more of it. But I know it's not for everyone, and I would hardly be one to say it ought to be. Plus, even if psychology were to more readily embrace first-person accounts, there would still, for most, be the task of "representing" these accounts in some way through writing and theorizing. Finally, it can plausibly be argued that psychology has had enough of the self,

DOI: 10.4324/9780429323652-8

that it is entirely too individualistic and ego-centric, and, as was suggested in the previous chapter, that it ought to be decidedly more Other-directed or "ex-centric" (Freeman, 2012, 2014a; Goodman & Freeman, 2015). Can the need for a more fully realized first-person psychology, focused on the self, be reconciled with the idea of a poetics of the Other? I believe it can. But I am not quite ready to say how yet. Instead, I want to explore more fully this idea of first-person psychology, including both the large challenges it entails and the large possibilities it brings forth.

Let me begin by turning once more to Gadamer's work. In *Truth and Method* (1975), he acknowledges that

> the discovery of the true meaning of a text or a work of art is never finished; it is in fact an infinite process. Not only are fresh sources of error constantly excluded, so that the true meaning has filtered out of it all kinds of things that obscure it, but there emerge continually new sources of understanding, which reveal unsuspected elements of understanding. The temporal distance that performs the filtering process is not a closed dimension, but is itself undergoing constant movement and extension. And with the negative side of the filtering process brought about by temporal distance there is also the positive side, namely the value it has for understanding. It not only lets those prejudices that are of a particular and limited nature die away, but causes those that bring about genuine understanding to emerge clearly as such.
>
> (pp. 265–266)

As Gadamer goes on to state,

> It is only this temporal distance that can solve the really critical question of hermeneutics, namely of distinguishing the true prejudices, by which we understand, from the false ones by which we misunderstand. Hence the historically trained mind will also include historical consciousness [and] will make conscious the prejudices governing our own understanding, so that the text, as another's meaning, can be isolated and valued on its own.
>
> (p. 266)

So far, so good: Gadamer's perspective here is in keeping with what was said back in Chapter 2 and helps to show that, appearances notwithstanding, it is our very belonging in and to history, replete with the prejudices that comprise it, that is the condition of possibility for our understanding. The same basic idea may be applied to the history that is our own: The project of self-understanding, far from emerging out of some place of neutrality (would that it were possible), has as its condition of possibility our own belonging in and to history—including both our life history and the larger history within which our life assume its distinctive form.

But what is self-understanding? And how do we know when we are attaining it? I cannot help but return to a quip that a good friend of mine offered when I posed this very question to him many years ago. "It's easy," he said. "I feel bad." There may be some truth to this idea. Oftentimes, the search for self-understanding and self-knowledge issues from a conflict or problem of some sort, or a felt disjunction between what is and what ought to be, and the challenge is to look candidly at oneself in order to determine what might be going on. The challenge is large. Some of the prejudices we bring to the task may be "bad" ones; we may distort the past owing to what we cannot, or will not, see; we may "sweeten" it, even if unconsciously, in order to shield ourselves from our own faults and foibles; and, not least, we may "overstory" it, as it were, skate over some of its subtleties and nuances and contradictions in the service of telling a coherent tale. The challenge is so large, in fact, that some have argued that the stories we tell about and to ourselves are ultimately fictions—as are we.

There is some validity to this stance. There is, for instance, the fact that "You are the only one who can never see yourself except as an image" (Barthes, 1989, p. 36). "One cannot really see one's own exterior," Bakhtin (1986) adds, "and no mirrors or photographs will help." The fact is, "our real exterior can be seen and understood only by other people, because they are located outside us and because they are *others*" (p. 7). In encountering our own selves, we must therefore emulate these others in a way, and thereby see "oneself as another" (Ricoeur, 1992). But of course the "me" the "I" encounters when we pursue the project of self-understanding (James, 1950 [1890]) is *not* "another," and try as we might to see ourselves as we would someone else, there is no escaping the aforementioned fact that the very "text" we seek to interpret and understand is, in a very real sense, one of our own makings; it is part of us, and thus does not, and cannot, stand alone and apart, like the books on our bookshelves (Freeman, 1997). So, here is the situation we have at hand. In exploring some facet of myself, "I" bring my language, my storehouse of culturally fashioned understandings and narrative patterns, and my current psychological situation, with its sundry wishes, needs, and defenses, both conscious and unconscious. As for the particular aspect of "me," I am seeking to understand at this particular moment in time—which is essentially a memorial image I have fashioned, issuing from the present moment, likely to assume the form of a somewhat blurry montage, comprising elements of both "then" and "now," firsthand material and second-hand material, memory and fantasy—it is itself suffused with all of this prejudicial matter as well. The result of this I/me encounter is likely to be a story of some sort, one that somehow gathers together the various elements and episodes of my life into some more or less singular narrative (Freeman, 2010). How, then, could the resultant product *not* be a fiction? And what place could there possibly be in this rendition of things for the "truth"?

Consider in this context what the literary theorist Georges Gusdorf has to say about this issue in his classic article "Conditions and limits of autobiography" (1980 [1956]). The difficulty is inevitable and insurmountable:

> no trick of presentation even when assisted by genius can prevent the narrator from always knowing the outcome of the story he tells—he commences, in a manner of speaking, with the problem already solved. Moreover, the illusion begins from the moment that the narrative confers a meaning on the event which, when it actually occurred, no doubt had several meanings or perhaps none. This postulating of a meaning dictates the choice of the facts to be retained and of the details to bring out or to dismiss according to the demands of the preconceived intelligibility. It is here that the failures, the gaps, and the deformations of memory find their origin; they are not due to purely physical cause nor to chance, but on the contrary they are the result of an option of the writer who remembers and wants to gain acceptance for this or that revised and corrected version of his past, his private reality.
>
> (p. 42)

Ultimately, therefore, Gusdorf asserts,

> The significance of autobiography should . . . be sought beyond truth and falsity, as those are conceived by simple common sense. It is unquestionably a document about a life, and the historian has a perfect right to check out its testimony and verify its accuracy. [But] it is of little consequence that the *Mémoires d'outretombe* should be full of errors, omissions, and lies, and of little consequence also that Chateaubriand made up most of his *Voyage en Amérique*: the recollection of landscapes that he never saw and the description of the traveller's moods nevertheless remain excellent. We may call it fiction or fraud, but its artistic value is real: there is a truth affirmed beyond the fraudulent itinerary and chronology, a truth of the man, images of himself and of the world, reveries of a man of genius, who, for his own enchantment and that of his readers, realizes himself in the unreal.
>
> (p. 43)

For Gusdorf, "The literary, artistic function is thus of greater importance than the historic or objective function in spite of the claims made by positivist criticism both previously and today" (p. 43). The person who sets out to answer the "Who am I?" question "does not surrender to a passive contemplation of his private being. The truth is not a hidden treasure, already there, that one can bring out by simply reproducing it as it is." No; discerning the past "realizes itself as a work in the present: it effects a true creation of the self by the self." The implication: "The creative and illuminating nature thus discerned in autobiography suggests a new and more profound sense of truth as an expression of inmost being, a likeness no longer of things but of the person" (p. 44). And this likeness, one can presume, is that which the autobiographer posits between their self-image and the story told; "it does not show us the individual seen from the outside in his visible actions but the person in his inner privacy, not as he was, not as he is, but as he believes and wishes himself to be and have been" (p. 45). Much the same, it might be held, can be said of the self more generally: It is a self-fashioned self-image; and, like autobiography, its significance should be sought "beyond truth and falsity," as Gusdorf had put it, at least "as conceived by simple common sense."

What exactly is this "simple common sense"? On a very basic level, it entails the assumption that "truth" has to do with what is unassailably "factual" and that "falsity" or "fictionality" has to do with virtually everything else. So it is the neuroscientist Michael Gazzaniga (1998), for instance, can proclaim that autobiography is "hopelessly inventive" (p. 2) and that it cannot help but result in *lies*. In order to "keep our personal story together," he writes,

> we have to learn to lie to ourselves. . . . We need something that expands the actual facts of our experience into an ongoing narrative, the self-image we have been building in our mind for years. The spin doctoring that goes on keeps us believing that we are good people, that we are in control and mean to do good. It is probably the most amazing mechanism the human being possesses.
>
> (pp. 26–27)

Gazzaniga's conclusion: "Sure, life is a fiction, but it's our fiction and it feels good and we are in charge of it" (p. 172). Putting aside the question of whether these "fictions" always "feel good," what we have in Gazzaniga and others of his ilk is a modern, neuroscientifically inspired version of Gusdorf's thesis, the latter's portrait of the autobiographer spinning yarns in accordance with what "he believes and wishes himself to be and have been" having been transformed into the former's fiction-and-feel-good liar, whose very identity is grounded in "the illusion that we are something other than what we are" (p. 175).

It may be that some aspects of Gazzaniga's perspective are valid. But philosophically, he succumbs to exactly that truth/falsity binary referred to before. We do, however, have a problem before us. If the stories we tell and the selves we are neither "objectively" truthful, in the way Gazzaniga has framed them, and if, consequently, there is a fictive, if not outright fictional element, to both, what value can such stories possibly have for psychology? Is truth just out the window? Or, perhaps we can just think of truth in the first-person context as a subjective truth—*my* truth, as it's sometimes called? Maybe in some circumstances, this is okay; maybe the story I tell myself "works" for me, helps me get on in the world, and allows me to frame myself in positive terms, like both Gusdorf and Gazzaniga said. Philosophically, however, this doesn't quite work, and it's not clear how well it works psychologically either, except in extreme cases. Think of Donald Trump. (I apologize for asking you to do so.) In his (bizarre) eyes, he is a self-made man, a winner, and his history is a string of victories. He's brilliant, a genius, someone who knows everything there is to be known about everything. (I'll stop.) Much of this is patently false. Does *he* know it's patently false? Good chance not; it seems that there is nothing, *nothing*, that could falsify the story he tells himself and the self-image he's created. Is it possible that he *dreams* something closer to the truth, or that he sometimes catches himself in the act of his own pathetic fibs and admits, "You really are a loser. And a jerk"? Also good chance not. But he is truly an extreme case. The more important point, in any case, is that we see here, in the patent falsity of his story and self-image, an implicit pointer toward the truth—that is, the fact that he's a loser and a jerk who is utterly deluded about who and what he is. And if we can identify patent falsity, we must be able to discern, or at least posit, some form of truth.

There is something else that pushes in the direction of truth as well. Were Donald Trump a less extreme case, perhaps he would, at times, look back at some aspect of his past, find his own rendition of it wanting, and by identifying it as such, begin to move toward the truth. But what can it possibly be? Is there a way of reimagining the idea of truth, in the human context, even amidst the "constraints" we have been considering?

Owen Flanagan (1996) has some useful things to say about these issues. On his account, it is important to distinguish two different aims tied to the process of self-representation:

> First, there is self-representation for the sake of self-understanding. This is the story we tell ourselves to understand ourselves for who we are. The ideal here is convergence between self-representation and an acceptable version of the story of our actual identity. Second, there is self-representation for public dissemination, whose aim is underwriting successful social interaction. The two are closely connected. Indeed, the strategic requirements of the sort of self-representation needed for social interaction, together with our tendencies to seek congruence, explain how self-representation intended in the first instance for "my eyes only," and thus, one might think, more likely to remain true, could start to conform to a false projected social image of the self, to a deeply fictional and far-fetched account of the self.
>
> (pp. 68–69)

As Flanagan (1996) goes on to suggest—rightly, I think, if controversially—"Self-represented identity, when it gets things right, has actual identity (or some aspect of it) as its cognitive object." Why controversially? We have already seen some of the difficulties inherent in the idea of "getting things right." In a related vein, it is no simple task to speak of one's "actual identity." One might even ask: *Is* there such a thing? It might be possible to speak of one's actual "personality," that is, that which might be measured or observed by others in some sort of "objective" way. But insofar as my identity is *mine*, it is not entirely clear whether a comparable move can be made. In the end, again, aren't I just whatever I make myself out to be, however distorted and deranged my own self-representation may be? Isn't this notion of self-making (Bruner, 1987, 1991) ultimately what identity, especially "narrative identity" (McAdams & McLean, 2013; Ricoeur, 1992; Singer, 2004), is all about?

The answer is clear: Yes and no. Yes; the narratives I tell about myself and to myself are, in part, constitutive of my identity. This is true, Flanagan (1996) tells us, in two senses:

> First, even considered as a purely cognitive activity, self-representation involves the activation of certain mental representations and cognitive structures. Once self-representation becomes an ongoing activity, it realigns and recasts the representations and structures already in place. Second, the self as represented has motivational bearing and cognitive effects. Often, this motivational bearing is congruent with motivational tendencies that the entire system already has. Sometimes, [however], especially in cases of severe self-deception, the self projected for both public and first-person consumption may be strangely and transparently out of kilter with what the agent is like. In such cases, the self as represented is linked with the activity of self-representation but with little else in the person's psychological and behavioral economy. Nonetheless, such misguided self-representation helps constitute . . . the misguided person's actual full identity.
>
> (p. 69)

Has the aforementioned dilemma been resolved? Not yet. As Flanagan (1996) himself acknowledges,

> To conceive of the self as a fiction seems right for four reasons: it is an open-ended construction; it is filled with vast indeterminate spaces, and a host of tentative hypotheses about what I am like, that can be filled out and revised post facto; it is pinned on culturally relative narrative hooks; and it expresses ideals of what one wishes to be but is not yet.
>
> (pp. 72–73)

At the same time, he quickly adds, the self-as-fiction idea is "misleading" too. For one, "The author of a true piece of fiction has many more degrees of freedom in creating her characters than we have in spinning the tales of our selves. . . . There are, after all, the things we have done, what we have been through as embodied social beings, and the characteristic dispositions we reveal in social life." As such, "Third parties will catch us if we take our story too far afield." What's more, if we are truly forthright in our self-encounters, "We may also catch ourselves." For Flanagan, "There are selection pressures," as he calls them, "to keep the story one reveals to oneself and to others in some sort of harmony with the way one is living one's life." Second, as we noted earlier, "some people . . . are massively self-deceived," and, as we also noted, "self-deception only makes sense if selves are not totally fictive, that is, only if there are some facts constraining what is permitted in our self narrative. So real selves are fictional to a point. But they are less fictional than fictional selves because they are more answerable to the facts. The self," therefore, "can be a construct or model, a 'center of narrative gravity,' a way of self-representation, without being a fiction in the problematic sense" (p. 73).

One could quibble with Flanagan's reference to "the facts." One could also quibble with his recourse to the language of "representation." But let us not quibble. Instead, let us dive deeper into the dilemma before us. On the one hand, insofar as the self is an "open-ended construction, . . . filled with vast indeterminate spaces, and a host of tentative hypotheses about what I am like, that can be filled out and revised post facto," and is also "pinned on culturally relative narrative hooks," expressing "ideals of what one wishes to be but is not yet," we would appear to be far (far) away from considering the "truth" of selfhood as anything but a purely subjective one. On the other hand, we are, on Flanagan's account, as well as my own, "constrained" by the fleshy particulars of our lives, and it is patently clear that, even if there is no promised identity land of unvarnished truth, there is an all too vast landscape of falsity and self-deception, which, in turn, would seem to imply that there must also be a condition of *un*-self-deception—a "region" of truth, as I referred to it earlier (Freeman, 2002c, 2010).

So yes, the stories we tell about ourselves, and to ourselves, are extremely important. They are indeed constitutive of who we are, formative of our very identities. This is precisely why it might be argued that who I am, as a self, is what I take myself narratively to be. But we—or at least I—cannot rest comfortably in this position. It is simply too subjective. Plus, I think there are more truthful ways of speaking to the reality of selfhood, such as it is. It's not that I can't tell a story about this phase of my life, or at least certain aspects of it. I also think that some insights, even truths, might issue from the process. But more and more, I have come to see just how fragile this process is and what a profound challenge it is to discern who and what we are and how we might have become that. Alongside the narrative we might consciously bring to mind based on what we know and believe about our past, there is, I would hold, another, deeper narrative—or would-be narrative, tied to unspeakable events like fathers' early deaths, or "spectacular" (as the newspaper put it) car crashes like the one I was in at age 17, or loves gone south—not to mention, of course, all of the Freudian dark matter circulating through the nether reaches of our childhoods, resonating in ways we might barely acknowledge, if at all.

I don't mean to suggest that only negative or painful experiences are the ones with lasting but difficult-to-discern consequences. There are positive ones too, and ordinary ones that happen our way during the course of a day or month or year. These too seep into the psychical bloodstream in ways largely unbeknownst to us. There is no reconstructing them in any definite way, no charting them. In addition, there are, as noted earlier, dimensions of our lives that are rooted in history and culture and are part of the deep, largely unconscious, backdrop of being (Freeman, 2002a, 2010) and that comprise those culturally rooted aspects of our histories that have yet to become—and may never become—an explicit part of our stories. In this context too, therefore, there is thus no "getting around" the reality before us, especially insofar as it is absent the kind of solidity we frequently encounter in realities outside of ourselves. All we can do, then, is interpret and narrate. But how?

Karl Ove Knausgaard addresses this very question in the aforementioned book *Inadvertent* (2018). "We live in an ocean of time," he writes,

> where events, things, and people are continually succeeding one another, but we cannot live with such boundless complexity, because we disappear in it, and therefore we organize it into categories, sequences, hierarchies. We organize ourselves—I am not nameless, my name is such and such, my parents were like this and that, I went to school in such and such a place, I experienced this and that, by character I am like this and like that, and that has caused me to choose this and that. And we organize our surroundings—we don't just live on a plain with some grass, bushes, roads, and houses, we live in a particular place in a particular country with a particular culture, and we belong to a particular stratum within that culture.
>
> All of us sum up our lives in this way, that is what we call identity; and we sum up the world we inhabit in similar ways that is what is called culture. What we are saying about ourselves fits, but no more than if we had said something entirely different, thought something entirely different about ourselves and our place in the world—if, for example, we had lived during the Middle Ages and not in the early twenty-first century—and it too would have fit and seemed meaningful.
>
> (pp. 10–11)

What is the implication here? One implication is that the "fit" between our identity and our understanding of the world is, on some level, arbitrary. I don't think Knausgaard is right about this. That the kind of story I tell myself now couldn't possibly have been told in the Middle Ages is surely so, but that doesn't make it arbitrary. On the contrary, this story has a kind of necessity, tied to the lifeworld I have come to inhabit, the kinds of selves that are born into this world, and the kinds of understandings, and misunderstandings, that circulate through it.

This is where the interpretive challenge begins. For Knausgaard, it is also where *writing* begins. The reason, as he told us back in Chapter 5, is that "literature by its very nature always seeks complexity and ambiguity" and thereby rejects "monologic claims of truth about the world" (p. 11)—including, especially, the world of selfhood. The point is an important one. If Knausgaard is right, the most appropriate inroad into discerning the self, in all of its mystery and multiplicity, is through literature, literary *poiesis*—and, I would add, those other modes of *poiesis* found throughout the various arts.

The challenge at hand is a massive one—one in fact that cannot ever fully be met. For, even amidst the inevitable cultural-historical situatedness and saturatedness that characterize the stories we tell about ourselves, it is imperative, still, to find language that, in some way, transcends this very condition. "Writing," Knausgaard asserts,

> is precisely about disregarding how something seems in the eyes of others, it is precisely about freeing oneself from all kinds of judgments and from posturing and positioning. Writing is about making something accessible, allowing something to reveal itself.
>
> (p. 27)

"Thoughts," therefore—or at least those thoughts that are rooted in these conventionalized judgments—"are the enemy of the inadvertent, for if one thinks about how something will seem to others,"—or, I would add, to oneself—"if one thinks about whether something is important or good enough, if one begins to calculate and to pretend, then it is no longer inadvertent and accessible as itself, but only as what we have made it into" (p. 28).

Knausgaard adopts something of a "method" to counteract all this—

> a method in which I simply wouldn't have time to think, to plan or to calculate, I would have to go with whatever appeared on the screen in front of me. This method came about because I had set out to write about myself, and since we know more about ourselves than about any other subject, it seemed important to avoid the established versions and to seek instead the complexity that lies beneath our self-insight and self-image and which can be accessed only by not thinking about how our thoughts and feelings will seem to others, how it will look, who I am if I think and feel these things.
>
> This form made it possible to see how closely interwoven the "I" is with the "we," how language, culture, and our collective notions course through us, how common even our most secret and solitary emotions are. I hadn't realized that before, nor did I expect to as I set out to write these books, for then my idea was to write about the most private of matters, that which was only my own, while what the form I had chosen enabled me to say turned out in the end to be the very opposite.
>
> (pp. 37–38)

Hence the importance of the idea of the inadvertent:

> I have to hit upon it inadvertently, or it has to hit upon me. It is one thing to know something, another to write about it, and often knowing stands in the way of writing. *Make it new*, Ezra Pound said—and is there any other way to do that than to let everything we know about something fall away and regard it from a position of defenselessness and unknowing?
>
> (p. 40)

Following Knausgaard in broad outline, it would appear that we have before us both a large challenge and a quite radical opportunity to rethink and reimagine the project of exploring and discerning the self. In his view, who and what we are is inevitably bathed in obscurity, partly because our own "notions about the world" cannot help but constrain our capacity to discern what is really there and partly because our own defensive, ego-driven designs cannot help but intrude on our own capacity to truly know ourselves. We therefore arrive at what may appear to be a very odd premise for an inquiry into selfhood: In order to fathom the mystery of identity, it is imperative, once more, that we "unself" ourselves (Murdoch, 1970), in such a way as to allow whatever we may have "kept down," whether wittingly or unwittingly, to "rise to the surface." The most appropriate vehicle for doing so, on this account, is *literature*, artful writing that seeks to disclose or "unconceal" (Heidegger, 1971) that in ourselves which had heretofore been obscured or opaque.

Let me briefly review the territory we have covered thus far in the form of three interrelated ideas. First, while the stories we tell about ourselves, and to ourselves, are not arbitrary, the process of telling these stories is, as I put it earlier, extremely fragile, in the sense of being highly susceptible to conventionalized understandings. This susceptibility is all but inevitable. As Ernst Schachtel (1959) has stated,

> In the course of later childhood, adolescence, and adult life, perception and experience . . . develop increasingly into the rubber stamps of conventional clichés. The capacity to see and feel what is there gives way to the tendency to see and feel what one expects to see and feel, which, in turn, is what one is expected to see and feel because everybody else does. Experience increasingly assumes the form of the cliché under which it will be recalled because this cliché is what conventionally is remembered by others.
>
> (p. 288)

The same is true of memory, which "is even more governed by conventional patterns than are perception and experience" (p. 291), and most important for present purposes, the same is true of the stories we might ultimately tell about our lives. Along these lines, Schachtel, not unlike Knausgaard, notes that "the greatest problem of the writer or the poet is the temptation of language. At every step a word beckons, it seems so convenient, so suitable, one has heard or read it so often in a similar context"—an already *known* context. It is imperative, therefore, "to fight constantly against the easy flow of words that offer themselves" and to thus enter into the unknown. Ultimately, Schachtel acknowledges, there is no way to fully move beyond the culturally, and linguistically, articulated world we inhabit. He also acknowledges that "the endeavor to articulate, express, and communicate an experience can never succeed completely" (p. 296). Yet, one must move in this direction as best one can. Following Knausgaard and Schachtel, the first and perhaps most basic challenge of exploring and discerning the self is precisely to find language that somehow counteracts our susceptibility to those narrative scripts and schemes that inevitably "beckon" us, luring us into the too-comfortable confines of predigested modes of thinking, feeling, and writing. It is a tall order.

As we have also noted, the stories we tell about ourselves, and to ourselves, are susceptible to the consolations, and, at times, outright illusions we may unwittingly hold as well as the lure of rational "understanding." By virtue of such consolations and illusions, along with this rationalizing process, aiming as it does toward comprehension and grasping, our deeper corridors are, to a greater or lesser extent, occluded. They thus warrant hermeneutic "suspicion" (Ricoeur, 1970, 1974), and call for strategies of laying bare, or at least barer, these deeper corridors. Having said this, we ought not to operate under the further illusion that we can reach transparency. Freud's aspirations notwithstanding, there *is* no making the unconscious conscious—not fully at any rate. It is, once more, that which is not to be gotten around. The mystery, the irreducible mystery, thus remains. Our origins, in their vast multiplicity, reach down into the unknown, and there is no getting to them, certainly not with any precision, no means by which we can reach the rock bottom of transparent understanding. This is not to be seen as some sort of interpretive failure, however. On the contrary, it is simply an avowal of what I referred to earlier as interpretive humility, including a willingness to say the words, "I don't know." What we are after, therefore, is a different kind of knowing than the kind we often take to the world, one which is not a grasping but is instead a kind of *unknowing*, as Knausgaard had put it. This unknowing, I suggest, is critical to the project of exploring and discerning the self.

You may recall that "funk" I described back in Chapter 2. Do I have any significant clues for what it was all about? I do, actually, and with time and distance, I may have more. Finally, though, *I don't know*. And strictly speaking, I *can't* know. Instead, I need to "erode my own notions about the world," as Knausgaard put it, and see what emerges. This, we have seen, means "[abdicating] as king of myself and "[letting] the literary, in other words writing and the forms of writing, lead the way." Even with this more methodical approach, however, I would not, and could not, have arrived at clear and clean answers to the questions I might have posed—especially the overarching question: Who am I? One reason, again, is that the self, rather than being an object in the world, may be better understood as a kind of "presence," as Marcel (1950) had put it, an ungraspable reality calling for a different mode of apprehension than objects permit. But even this may not be quite right. The reason, as we have also noted, is because when "I" encounter "me," there is nothing truly *there*—save the somewhat gauzy, ethereal image I myself fashion as I seek to come to terms with this or that aspect of my life. If we are to speak of "presence," therefore, it is a ghostly one at best, an absent presence, as it were, something that is at once eminently real yet wholly ungraspable.

That psychologists have sought to "contain" the self in one way or another stands to reason; it is important, at times, to get hold of what we can. But it is equally important, I think, to recognize and avow the existence of phenomena that resist this getting hold and that therefore require something else, something better suited to the phenomena in question. In the case of selfhood, at least as understood in first-person terms, this something is literature (Freeman, 2020). Just like us, works of literature have beginnings, middles, and endings. Just like us, they are characterized by a kind of spiraling hermeneutic motion, wherein we, as readers, tack back and forth between episodes and evolving plot, which in turn conditions the meaning both of past episodes and those to come. Just like us, works of literature are essentially "open," there to interpret as best we can. Even if we aren't works of literature, of the sort we find on our bookshelves, therefore, we are certainly neighbors, kindred spirits. It should therefore come as no great surprise that, when we really want to dig into the depths of personal being, we curl up with a good book. I would hardly want to restrict ourselves to literature alone, however. For there are other arts, and other domains beyond the arts, that can also be profoundly instructive in disclosing to us who and what we are—or might be. These too are the domain of the psychological humanities, and it is imperative that we clear an adequate space for them going forward.

8 A Space for the Ineffable

You may recall how enchanted I was when I came across William James's (1950 [1890]) call for "the re-instatement of the vague to its proper place in our mental life" (p. 254). Vintage James, to be sure. Shortly after, I voiced a related enchantment when I mentioned his (1982 [1890]) conviction that, when it comes to the domain of religious experience especially, "the claims of the sectarian scientist"—to essentially explain away religious experience by rendering it, or trying to render it, in wholly scientific terms—are "premature" (p. 122). Why not let such experiences speak in their own terms, and why not fashion ways of accounting for and depicting such experiences that truly do justice to them?

Easier said than done, of course. One problem, interestingly enough, is not unrelated to the one we considered in the previous chapter. As James notes in his chapter on "The reality of the unseen" from *The Varieties of Religious Experience* (1982 [1902]), "It is as if there were in the human consciousness *a sense of reality, a feeling of objective presence, a perception* of what we may call *'something there,'* more deep and more general than any of the special and particular 'senses' by which the current psychology supposes existent realities to be originally revealed" (p. 58). This is especially so in certain forms of religious experience. It's possible that such experiences are merely hallucinatory, psychical realities projected outward with such force and form that they are deemed to be outside the self. Either way, "the person affected will feel a 'presence' in the room, definitely localized, facing in one particular way, real in the most emphatic sense of the word, often coming suddenly, and as suddenly gone; and yet neither seen, heard, touched, nor cognized in any of the usual 'sensible' ways" (p. 59). We therefore "have the strange phenomenon . . . of a mind believing with all its strength, in the real presence of a set of things of no one of which it can form any notion whatsoever" (p. 55). In fact,

> The sentiment of reality can indeed attach itself so strongly to our object of belief that our life is polarized through and through, so to speak, by its sense of the existence of the thing believed in, and yet that thing, for purpose of definite description, can hardly be said to be present to our mind at all.
>
> (p. 55)

DOI: 10.4324/9780429323652-9

Shades of the self!

The challenge here, though, takes us into still deeper waters. For when it comes to phenomena like religious experience, aesthetic experience, and other such spheres of the ineffable (and, perhaps, invisible), it is also often held that the experiences in question bespeak the existence of a realm of reality that may be "transcendent" in nature—that is, a reality of a different kind than may be revealed by "any of the special and particular 'senses'." For the most part, psychology hasn't quite known what to do with such experiences and has tended to leave them largely uncharted. And when it has tried to take on such experiences—perhaps through "peak experiences" (Maslow, 1970), "flow" (Csikszentmihalyi, 1990), and other such accounts—it has often done so in a naturalistic way, grounded in the assumption—or, more accurately, *pre*sumption—that, ontologically speaking, the phenomena in questions are ultimately like any other natural phenomena and that, consequently, they are to be approached in scientific terms, difficult though it may be to do so with the desired precision.

James himself held to this basic stance in *The Varieties* by trying to account for religious experience in naturalistic, wholly secular terms as far as it seemed possible. Rather than immediately leaping into the metaphysical or "spiritual" sphere, he went as far as he could to account for it scientifically. In one sense, James (1982) notes in the chapter on conversion, psychology and religion are "in perfect harmony . . ., since both admit that there are forces seemingly outside of the conscious individual that bring redemption to his life." But psychology, "defining these forces as 'subconscious,' and speaking of their effects as due to 'incubation,' or 'cerebration,' implies that they do not transcend the individual's personality." At this point, therefore, "she diverges from Christian theology,"—among other theologies—"which insists that they are direct supernatural operations of the Deity." James then goes on to propose "that we do not yet consider the divergence final, but leave the question for a while in abeyance" (p. 211). By the book's end, this question is still in abeyance, though there are some quite robust clues about how he is inclined to address it.

Can there be an approach to the kinds of experiences James is exploring, within the confines of psychology, that allows for the possibility that the forces felt to be operative *do* transcend the individual's personality? And if so, can it allow for the further, and more provocative, possibility that these forces may have a truly transcendent source—by which I mean one that entails "higher spiritual energies," as James puts it, of some sort? And if *this* is so, mightn't it also be the case that psychology ought to find a suitable space for such phenomena, one that is, of necessity, beyond the purview of science, as customarily conceived? For thinkers like Flanagan (or least the Flanagan [2003]) I referred to back in Chapter 1, and also Dawkins (2008), Harris (2005), and numerous others, the answer to all of these questions would seem to be a firm and unequivocal "No." Why? Because the very *a priori* assumptions with which they are operating prohibit any other answer. They may still want to "honor" such experiences, and they may even avow that some special, humanities-type language may be required to speak to them given their ostensibly ineffable nature. But if in fact one believes, through and through, that science is (to put it crudely) "the only game in town," then any and all experiences of the sort we have been considering must, of necessity, be considered natural and thus amenable to scientific understanding.

As I began to think more about the direction this chapter was taking, I realized that I was returning to my interest (Freeman, 2014a, 2014d) in "defending" the idea of transcendence, especially in the face of those who ruled it completely out of bounds (which includes virtually all of psychology). I am going to keep what I have written here; I think it's important, and provides some context for the ideas to follow. But my interest here, now, is different. Whether transcendence is "real" or not—for simplicity's sake, whether it speaks some sort of spiritual or even divine connection (see Kearney, 2001, 2010); Murdoch, 1970)—the experience remains what it is. Elaine Scarry (1999) speaks to this very issue. In experiencing beauty, for instance, the object in question not only "fills the mind" but "invites the search for something beyond itself, something larger or something of the same scale with which it needs to be brought into relation" (p. 29). Whether or not this "something" truly exists in some immortal, transcendent sphere is, in a certain sense, irrelevant:

> Even when the claim on behalf of immortality is gone, many of the same qualities—plenitude, inclusion—are the outcome. . . . What happens when there is no immortal realm behind the beautiful person or thing is just what happens when there *is* an immortal realm behind the beautiful person or thing: the perceiver is led to a more capacious regard for the world.
>
> (pp. 47–48)

The perceiver may be led to a greater sense of *connection* as well: This world that comes before me, one may feel, is much larger than me, but it is also one to which I belong. Such experience thus understood becomes a kind of *homecoming*, as I (Freeman, 2014a) have called it, wherein one's very belongingness in and to the world is revealed in and through its commanding presence. It may be that this experience of belongingness to some larger sphere of reality or being is tied to the ecstatic quality that frequently accompanies it: "Insofar as the world is revealed as home, as the place where I belong, I am 'at one' with it, able, if only momentarily, to move beyond the condition of ordinary oblivion against which the experience is juxtaposed" (Freeman, 2014a, p. 171).

George Steiner (1989, 1997) says something similar in his discussion of musical experience. "The energy that is music," he writes,

> puts us in felt relation to the energy that is life; it puts us in a relation of experienced immediacy with the abstractly and verbally inexpressible but wholly palpable, primary fact of being. The translation of music into meaning . . . carries with it what somatic and spiritual cognizance we can have of the core-mystery (how else is one to put it?) that we are. And that this energy of existence lies deeper than any biological or psychological determination.
>
> (1989, p. 196)

Such experience, he continues, "mocks analytic rationalization" and "rebukes the arrogance of positivism, of the demand for a quantifiable, for a psychologically evidential or sociologically mapped explanation of things" (p. 217). In carrying intimations within it of a "radical 'non-humanity'," as he puts it, it immediately outstrips any wholly secular, scientific account of it we might give. He speaks of the embarrassment we sometimes feel "in bearing witness to the poetic, to the entrance into our lives of the mystery of otherness in art and in music." This mystery, he holds, along with James—"the reality of a presence, of a factual 'thereness' . . . defies either analytic or empirical circumscription" and bespeaks "a pressure of presence extra-territorial to explanation" (1997, p. 84).

Steiner, it should be noted, goes on to wonder whether "a hermeneutics . . . of valuation—the encounter with meaning in the verbal sign, in the painting, in the musical composition, and the assessment of the quality of such meaning in respect of form—can be made intelligible, can be made answerable to the existential facts, if they do not imply, if they do not contain, a postulate of transcendence" (1989, p. 134). His conviction is that they cannot, for the kind of experience he is addressing, and the kind of presence it entails is, in his view, "of a metaphysical and indeed religious kind" (1989, p. 178). More important in the present context, in any case, is the idea that such experience cannot be gotten around and thus "rebukes the arrogance of positivism, of the demand for a quantifiable, for a psychologically evidential or sociologically mapped explanation of things." These are strong, defiant words. Let me soften them just a bit by simply saying that, by virtue of the potentially ecstatic depth and ineffability of such experience, the usual, explanatory ways practiced by most of psychologists and sociologists just don't make it.

In Hans-Georg Gadamer's (1986) essay "The Relevance of the Beautiful" (1986), he argues similarly that "[w]hen we take aesthetic satisfaction in something, we do not relate it to a meaning which could ultimately be communicated in conceptual terms" (p. 20). A major aim of the essay is to tease out the implications of this fact. "What," he asks, "is the importance and significance of this particular experience which claims truth for itself, thereby denying that the universality expressed by the mathematical formulation of the laws of nature is the only kind of truth?" (pp. 16–17). More fully:

> What is this truth that is encountered in the beautiful and can come to be shared? Certainly not the sort of truth or universality to which we apply the conceptual universality of the understanding. Despite this, the kind of truth that we encounter in the experience of the beautiful does unambiguously make a claim to more than subjective validity.
>
> (p. 18)

Otherwise, Gadamer maintains, it would have no binding value. This is emphatically not to claim that what is being considered is nonintellectual; "there is always some reflective and intellectual accomplishment involved" (p. 28), he emphasizes. Nevertheless, one of the defining features of art—and the kinds of experiences to which art objects give rise—is that it resists pure conceptualization. One other curious phenomenon, he goes on to note, is that certain works of art, music especially—the art generally deemed least conducive to explicit conceptualization—often emerge in experience not only as *meaningful* but *profound*, even revelatory. "What is it about a piece of music," Gadamer asks, "that allows us to say that it is rather shallow or . . . that it is truly great and profound? What accounts for the sense of quality here? Not a determinate relation to anything that we could identify in terms of meaning. Is there some obscure relationship with language at work here," such that we are encountering "traces of conceptual meaning" (p. 38)? It could be. But it is not clear how much this idea helps us in the case of certain kinds of atonal music, for instance, or certain kinds of nonrepresentational paintings, which systematically seek to obliterate any and all traces of this sort. So the mystery remains.

Here is a particularly memorable, and somewhat mystifying, example of exactly this, which I also discussed in a piece titled "How does the world become ecstatic? Notes on the hermeneutics of transcendence" (Freeman, 2021c). The site was an exhibit at the Museum of Fine Arts (MFA) in Boston called "STOP. LOOK. BREATHE," where there were several all-black paintings by Mark Rothko. Before viewing the paintings, I read a statement about them that hung on the wall of the exhibit that reads as follows:

> The world moves quickly. Here, we encourage you to pause—for Mark Rothko's paintings reward slow looking. Large, often bold or colorful, they are also extraordinarily subtle and nuanced. Frequently, Rothko created them with successive layers of thinned-down paint, resulting in effects of transparency, luminosity, texture, and depth that emerge through steady, open contemplation. Try one full minute in front of a canvas—it's longer than you think.

This was in keeping with my previous experiences with Rothko's work, many of which I had found extremely moving. I remember going to a Rothko exhibit at the Guggenheim in New York years earlier and being completely transfixed by his work, by their sheer sensuous presence. Why should it be? I wondered. It's just *paint*. Why should these pieces have the power they have?

As the writing on the wall of the MFA noted, Rothko himself had some definite ideas for how people should view his paintings. "He wanted us to first encounter them at close quarters—recommending, specifically, that we begin by standing 18 inches away from a large work. From there, the edges of the canvas fall into the periphery, and our experience would be of being within the painting." I went ahead and followed Rothko's directions. Not having seen these particular paintings before, I didn't know quite what to expect, and the fact of their being virtually all black (I eventually saw that there were some other dark colors in there too) complicated things, at least initially. I hadn't gotten much out of other "all-over" paintings I had seen in the past, and I didn't expect that this would be a whole lot different. But I don't know that I had ever had a more intensely moving experience with a painting than the one I had that day. I felt like I had entered the void, the black hole of the infinite, and I was suddenly beside myself in a kind of deep, ecstatic grief. I hesitate to say more about it; words—or at least the words I am sharing in this chapter—can't possibly do justice to what I had experienced.

"I became a painter," Rothko was quoted as saying, "because I wanted to raise painting to the level of poignancy of music and poetry." He was also quoted as saying, "The people who weep before my pictures are having the same religious experience I had when I painted them." Whether my experience warrants being called "religious" or "spiritual" remains open to question. But there is no question whatsoever about the sheer existential force of the experience itself.

I did go on to examine the possible sources of this experience, among others, in the (Freeman, 2021c) chapter I just mentioned. Here, I want just to consider the challenge of speaking to the experience itself. What exactly is to be said about this sort of experience? We do have at least one viable option here: Nothing! We could just leave it all alone! We can just groove on music, poetry, painting and all the rest and skip all of this wondering and questioning. When I'm playing guitar or listening to a great piece of music or being blown away by a great painting, that's exactly what I do. But it's not too long after that I sometimes find myself wondering and questioning once more. "What *was* that?" I might ask myself. And how might I speak to it? Here too, one could simply say: "Keeping wondering and questioning. Just keep it to yourself! After all, some of your go-to thinkers, like James, Steiner, and Gadamer, seem to pretty much agree that none of these experiences lend themselves to the kind of language psychologists tend to seek and employ." But all this means, in my view, is that we need a *different* kind of language, one that is more welcoming, open, and free—*poetic*, in a word. Why bother?

That's a tough question to answer. But I think there is one, and it's that finding a language that is adequate to religious experience, aesthetic experience, and other such ecstatic, seemingly transcendent forms of experience can allow us to share and to communicate dimensions of our own being that are often either undisclosed or "under wraps," ensconced within our own solitary souls. Finding the words to speak it can therefore bring people together, if only for a moment, united in their shared humanity. Speaking to this dimension of humanity, too, is part of the project of the psychological humanities. Let us therefore explore it further.

9 In the Service of Humanity (and Beyond)

Humanity. The word has two common meanings. The first has to do with being part of the human species, as in "all of humanity." The second has to do mainly with our relation to others, as in "her humanity really shone through." At the end of the previous chapter, I shared some words pertaining mostly to the former, as something we share—not just by virtue of being a member of the human species but also by being a member of the kind of species that can *feel* together, in our shared depths, and thereby allow us to be connected on a deeper plane. I have always liked how the Holy Cross mission statement puts it:

> Because the search for meaning and value is at the heart of the intellectual life, critical examination of fundamental religious and philosophical questions is integral to liberal arts education. Dialogue about these questions among people from diverse academic disciplines and religious traditions requires everyone to acknowledge and respect differences. Dialogue also requires us to remain open to that sense of the whole which calls us to transcend ourselves and challenges us to seek that which might constitute our common humanity.

This openness to the whole is very much a part of the vision I have been advocating, as is the aim of transcending ourselves and seeking our common humanity. My hope is that some of the work we do under the umbrella of the psychological humanities will support these aims.

It is, however, the second meaning of "humanity" that I most want to turn my attention to in this chapter. In some ways, I have already begun. In Chapter 4, for instance, I spoke of the idea of fidelity as entailing both the phenomenological dimension and the ethical, and in Chapter 6, when I did a deeper dive into the idea of fidelity to other persons, I spoke of the kind of "attitude" required by our engagement with them. Here, I want to say more about what it might mean to develop and foster our humanity, in the sense of our care for others. I also want to say something about what it might mean to develop and foster our care for the nonhuman world—animals, nature, and perhaps God, if one is inclined.

DOI: 10.4324/9780429323652-10

I see this chapter as something of a response to the kind of question that will inevitably be raised by some readers. What *use* is there to psychological humanities-style work? What *value?* With more traditional modes of psychological inquiry, the uses are quite clear: explanation, prediction, control, application to this or that phenomenon, and so on. There seems to be nothing quite like these in the kind of work I have been discussing in these pages. Indeed, as I have avowed elsewhere (Freeman, 2014b), some of this work is, arguably, positively *useless*. I will therefore offer a variant of William James's (1950 [1890]) clarion call for the reinstatement of the vague to its proper place in our mental life and in the psychology that seeks to do justice to it: May some of what we do be useless! May some of it be like a great work of art, which "inspires because it is separate, it is for nothing, it is for itself" and can thus serve "as an image of virtue" (Murdoch, 1993, p. 8).

The key to understanding this provocative idea is not to equate *value* with overt *utility*, in the sense of use value and instrumentality. As I put the matter in the piece just referred to (Freeman, 2014b), which was specifically about the value of qualitative inquiry,

> It may seem difficult to justify and defend this kind of work. It doesn't seek to predict and control. It may not yield profound implications for policy. And it may not seek to change the world—not directly, at any rate. This manifest uselessness notwithstanding, such inquiry surely possesses some measure of value, even virtue. For, having the opportunity to behold reality in its fullness—in this case, the reality of human lives, in all of their messiness and possible beauty—can serve to further humanize us and enlarge our understanding of who we are and what is possible. Indeed, just as art is sometimes said to be as much about the possible as the actual, so too with the stories we tell and the other forms of qualitative inquiry we pursue: They can awaken readers to other modes of life and, in so doing, can open up new regions of being. Alongside such awakening, qualitative inquiry, artfully crafted, can serve to strengthen such noble virtues as empathy, sympathy, and compassion. On the face of it, these two functions—the aesthetic and the ethical—may seem far removed from science, at least as customarily conceived. It might also seem like they don't have anything to do with applied issues, the world of practical affairs. But there is another way entirely to think about this issue. For, the more that qualitative inquiry can carry this aesthetic and ethical weight—the more it can evoke and appeal to readers by virtue of its depth and humanity—the more likely it is that they will care enough to want to do something on behalf of the people in question.
>
> (pp. 123–124)

This was one of the aims of the book on my mother. There, though, I didn't only speak to the possibility of people doing something, perhaps on behalf of their loved ones, I spoke to the possibility of people connecting with, or identifying with, some of what I said, and maybe finding a new way of looking at and relating both to their loved ones and to the phenomenon of dementia itself. Even in the absence of the book's overt utility, therefore, there might be value, human value. I hope so, anyway.

Such value can, of course, be present in those works of literature customarily considered part of the arts and humanities—memoirs and novels, for instance. Work in the psychological humanities tends to be somewhat different, though, in that it aspires to speak more explicitly about understanding and "appreciating" particular phenomena and seeking to relate them to some larger sphere of interest—in the book on my mother, to dementia, memory, personal identity, being a son, relationality. I have to be cautious in how I do so, of course; she is but a single "case," after all, and I am hardly in a position to present this one case as a stand-in for some larger population. At the same time, one case—or, more subtly, the words and actions of a single person—can say quite a lot.

One may nevertheless still ask: What distinguishes this kind of work from storytellers, poets, and other such full-fledged humanists? In one sense, this is an intellectual division-of-labor issue, and people are right to ask about it. I would actually have two answers. The first would be: sometimes, nothing at all—except for the context in which such work appears. Put a given piece of well-crafted narrative in a literary magazine, and it may be considered "creative nonfiction." Put it in an academic journal, where there might be a more explicit empirical or theoretical context within which the piece can be located, and it's a piece of qualitative science. The second answer—the one that may be more in keeping with something called "psychology"—is that there is a kind of generalizing, or even universalizing, dimension built in to the works of this sort. This implies that even in those instances where nothing at all is being explicitly done to draw out the relevant conclusions—for instance, when there is just plain narrative, resonant and beautiful, speaking to our spirit and heart—there can remain, immanent within the text, a dimension of meaning that exceeds its own particularity—or, put another way, a dimension of meaning that, within this very particularity, exceeds itself and thereby carries some value in relation to some larger sphere of interest. This value, again, is not so much *use* value as it is *human* value.

Let me offer another, quite different, example of what I am aiming at in this chapter, one tied to the political realm. In some of my most recent (Freeman, 2023) work, I have sought to address some of the uses and, especially, abuses of narrative. One of the main sources of this interest has been the way in which Donald Trump and his MAGA acolytes have used narrative for their own self-serving, generally nefarious, ends. At one point in my thinking about this issue, I thought it most important that some of us "fight narrative with narrative" and to do it with as much moral clarity and integrity as could possibly muster.

I knew the challenge was large. As CNN's former correspondent Brian Stelter (2018) had argued midway through Trump's presidential term, "President Trump is winning the story-telling game, with help from his friends in the media. . . . Watch enough of President Donald Trump's rallies," he said,

> and his power as a storyteller shines through. He's the hero, the savior, the dragon-slayer of his own story. The villains include Democrats, foreigners and the journalists in the back of the hall. Love him or hate him, but give credit where it's due: Trump is succeeding at telling a story. Trump's stories are often more fiction than fact. But the thing about a story, like a novel or a drama, is that it's not really meant to be fact-checked. The narrative is meant to make you *feel.*
>
> [my emphasis]

This struck me as an important point. Fighting corrupt narratives of this sort with more truthful and ethically defensible ones, grounded more in fact, evidence, and so on may well be necessary. But if Stelter is right, these more truthful, ethically defensible tellings and retellings can't be sufficient. At the time, I went on to note, the number of immigrants seeking to cross our southern border was down. Drugs tended to come in through legal ports of entry, not through secret border crossings and tunnels. The percentage of violent crimes was actually lower in the immigrant population than in the population of those born and raised in the U.S. There really *was* no crisis at the time—certainly not one of the magnitude that had been proclaimed. Much of this was common knowledge. But it didn't matter. Think about what it would have been like to strike back against Hitler's portrayal of the Jews with more truthful, ethically defensible tellings. "No; they're not like that. No; they weren't responsible for that. Here's the real story, the *true* story." Sad to say, these sorts of narrative "straightenings" wouldn't have mattered one whit—certainly not to those immovable defenders of the faith who already "knew" the truth.

As Stelter went on to point out, Trump's narratives tend to be about heroes and villains. "It's us versus them, darkness versus light." His lies are legendary. But many of them, Stelter emphasized,

> are in service of the grand story he's telling. Look past the lies for a moment, and you can see why his crowds love it. He says he's putting America first, fixing the economy, and fighting the dark forces trying to stop him. His story is about wall-building and swamp-draining and deep-state-defeating.

And "he is the hero," while the "pro-Trump media act as his co-producers. . . . In Hollywood terms, it's as if Trump has a well-stocked writers' room, where loyalists develop the plotlines for the next episodes."

As Stelter and others came to realize, the fact-checking, accountability journalism that was most often employed in responding to what had been going on turned out to be of finite value, mainly because people either didn't care about the truth, journalistically understood, or had all but abandoned it as a meaningful category (Kakutani, 2018; McIntyre, 2018). So, if we can't fight corrupt narratives with truth-telling corrections, I asked, what else is there? Were there other truth stories, other *kinds* of truth stories, that might be told? If so, of what sort? And here, I offered, it seemed important to follow Stelter's lead and return to the realm of *feeling*—or, more specifically, what might be called *ethically saturated feeling*. I am thinking especially of narratives, both nonfictional and fictional, that are, in their way, unassailable—not because of their factuality but because they speak, viscerally and compellingly, to the felt realities of human experience and, in so doing, call us out of ourselves, demanding our attention and care. I am thinking here once more of the kind of attention and care considered by thinkers like Levinas, whose aforementioned ideas about the face of the Other may serve to provide some direction.

I am also thinking about the tattoo one of our daughters, who is a hair stylist, has on her arm. I can't say I was thrilled when she told us she was getting one. Among other reasons, it was hard to predict what it would be. As it turned out, it depicted a scissors, shaped in the form of the "greater than" sign, along with the phrase, "Love is greater than fear." This struck me as very pertinent to the situation I was addressing. So much of the Trumpian narrative vision is bathed in fear—especially fear of the dangerous Other. The Other is thus *othered*, and with this othering, the face is eclipsed. Somehow, then, the face must be restored, and one way of doing so, I said, is to fashion narratives—counter-narratives, as it were—that yield different images, and different feelings, ones that are more about compassion and mercy and, ultimately, *love* than they are about fear and danger. In the context of immigrants crossing the border, for instance, there seemed to be nothing that could deter defenders of the need for tightening border security from the fear narrative—nothing, that is, until they heard stories, or saw images, of children being torn from the arms of their parents or locked in metal cages or even lying at the edge of a river, dead. For some, it's as if there had emerged a sudden realization: There are *people* involved here, vulnerable, suffering, despairing, and desperate.

Artfully told stories of this sort, whether nonfictional or fictional, may be important precisely because of their embodying ethically saturated feeling—feeling, and meaning, that exceed categories, conceptual containers, and stock storylines. I emphasize "artfully told." Given the limits of "setting the story straight" through some sort of fact-based journalistic accounting, it may be that such stories—we can add other artful forms too—are the soundest, most valuable response to some of the challenges and dangers being considered. Among the reasons for why this is so, artfully told stories and other artful forms, through their possible complexity, multivocality, and evocative power, can provide a counterweight to too-simple, too-unidimensional stories

(Adichie, 2009); they can expose and indict them for the mythical fictions they are and, in doing so, can point toward more adequate and indeed *truthful* renditions of things, especially those that restore the face of the Other, in *its* complexity, multivoicedness, and evocative power.

There is a twofold ethics at work here, both of which are in the service of humanity. The first has to do with this idea of restoring the face of those who have been *de*faced and indeed de-realized. Following Levinas, it is not only the Other that is being restored but also ourselves, our own humanity and humanness—now awakened and returned, now *remembered.* This broad way of thinking, however, ought not to be limited to our responsibility to, and for, the human world, for there is a vast world beyond the human that also demands our attention and care. I will not pretend to say anything substantive about this vast, nonhuman world; it hasn't been the focus of my work, and others (e.g., Farley, 1996; McKibben, 2006) have done much more than I possibly could to speak cogently to the issue. What I will say is that some of the work both being done and to be done, within the psychological humanities, can be of considerable value in awakening us to the realities, and needs, of the human as well as the nonhuman world. The main thing is that this work be done not out of fear but love.

10 Tear Down the Walls (in the Name of Love)

I don't know; I thought some revolution talk was called for, so I went with this chapter title. It probably sounds extreme to some, or maybe too destructive. But using the language of "opening the gates" or "spreading our wings" or some such thing didn't seem to suffice; it didn't carry the kind of energy, and urgency, that I felt as I penned this chapter. In addition, though, and more substantively, I do think that destruction and creation are of a piece, partners in reimagining and refashioning, whatever the object happens to be. In ushering a call to tear down the walls, therefore, I do so in this very spirit, armed with the hope that doing so can, and will, open up new modes of thinking, inquiring, and creating.

I told you in the first sentence of this book that what I was about to propose could be seen as "audacious." I even indicated that it probably was. I accept this and offer my apologies to those who think it's not only audacious but self-indulgent. "*His* vision. Who the f__k is he?"

I am no one. I am not any one thing. And the vision I have been setting forth in the previous pages is emphatically not mine, alone, but issues from all that has come before me, and all that I share with the good people whose work I have drawn upon, and all that I, we, may wish for in our own efforts to do better and to help create the kind of discipline, and the kind of home, we and our students can truly inhabit, be nourished by, and thrive in.

Some of the walls I am speaking of in this chapter are those that have been imposed by the discipline. But some of them are our own, internal walls too, partly internalized through our own disciplinary education and socialization and partly through our own possible desires to contain and explain, to *know*. These desires are worthy ones. Let us keep them alive! But let us not rest easy with them, alone, for they do entail a kind of wall, one that precisely *walls off* what cannot be contained, explained, and made known. One could argue, I suppose, that this sphere of the unknowable is but a fraction of the human experience. But it's not. How do I know this? Through every blessed day I have experienced in this world. I hardly think I am alone in this.

A day. What comprises one? As I sit in my room upstairs, strewn with books and plants and guitars and a bunch of sprays and creams for older

DOI: 10.4324/9780429323652-11

people (gulp), I am, right now, . . . moved, viscerally and spiritually. There is a kind of anxious energy coursing throughout my body. A part of me wants to explode. And a part of me wants to bask in silence and to feel. The latter part wins. I close my eyes and breathe, and live. I am immensely grateful, but in a subdued way, glad to be at home, glad to be home, to belong. It is a kind of grace. I am no one. Or something like it. There is only world, only Other. Or something close to it.

I am reminded of some of Simone Weil's (1997 [1952]) remarkable words. "Grace," she writes, "fills empty spaces but it can only enter where there is a void to receive it, and it is grace itself which makes this void" (p. 10). The aim, therefore, not unlike the one voiced earlier by Knausgaard (2018), is "to strip ourselves of the imaginary royalty of the world" (p. 12). Hence her fervent wish: "May I disappear in order that those things that I see become perfect in their beauty from the very fact that they are no longer things I see." As she clarifies, "I do not in the least wish that this created world should fade from my view, but that it should no longer be to me personally that it shows itself." She is well aware that this is impossible: "When I am in any place, I disturb the silence of heaven and earth by my breathing and the beating of my heart." But the aim remains: "to see a landscape as it is when I am not there" (p. 37)—in short, and to use Murdoch's (1970) words once more, to unself herself to the greatest possible extent in order to behold, and be beheld by, the world, in its radiant otherness.

This process about which Weil is speaking, of course, need not lead to the kind of work I have been describing in these pages. Unselfing, alone, is not sufficient. If she is right, however, it is necessary—at the ontological level (as discussed in Chapter 1), the interpretive level (as discussed in Chapter 2), and the reverential level (as discussed in Chapter 3). It is also necessary in establishing what I am herein calling a poetics (as in Chapter 4) of the Other (as in Chapter 5) as well as in the notion of fidelity—to others, to oneself, to the ineffable world, and to humanity (as in Chapters 6 through 9). If we are to tear down the walls, therefore, we must do so humbly, gently, with love.

Love. *Really?* Is that where all this leads? I can see some of my colleagues' eyes beginning to roll. "Freeman's gone off the deep end! Hardly unexpected, though." Fantasies aside, what might I mean by this term? Fidelity is certainly a part of it. Murdoch's (1970) work is especially helpful here. You may recall her idea that "true vision occasions right conduct," and that such true vision is entailed in works of art, or at least those works of art that "show us the world," particularly those features of it that may have gone unseen or under-seen. This brings us to the next step of her view. (I hesitate to call it an "argument."):

> If, still led by the clue of art, we ask further questions about the faculty which is supposed to relate us to what is real and thus bring us to what is good, the idea of compassion or love is naturally suggested. It is not simply that suppression of self is required before accurate vision can be

> obtained. The great artist sees his objects (and this is true whether they are sad, absurd, repulsive or even evil) in a light of justice and mercy. The direction of attention is, contrary to nature, outward, away from self which reduces all to a false unity, towards the great surprising variety of the world, and the ability to do so is love.
>
> (p. 65)

Murdoch's conclusion: "It is in the capacity to love, that is to *see*, that the liberation of the soul from fantasy consists. The freedom which is a proper human goal is the freedom from fantasy, that is the realism of compassion" (p. 65).

I have probably read these words 50 times, maybe more. But they continue to inform, and form, me. This time, they help me understand better what I seem to mean when I use the language of "walls." It is most obviously about freedom, the freedom from the kinds of constraints and prohibitions that characterize much of psychology, as well as the freedom to imagine and create. However, it is also about love, in the sense of seeing and beholding what is real, which is itself a precondition for discerning what is good—or, as Murdoch, following Plato, puts it, Good. Yes: "It is here that it seems to me to be important to retain the idea of Good as a central point of reflection, and here too we may see the significance of its indefinable and non-representable character" (p. 68). We thus return once more to "the reality of the unseen"—in this case, the deep, transcendent reality Murdoch associates with the Good. Tearing down the walls is thus to be done not only in the name of love but also, and necessarily, in the service of Good.

"Art and morals," Murdoch (1999) writes elsewhere,

> are . . . one. Their essence is the same. The essence of both of them is love. Love is the perception of individuals. Love is the extremely difficult realisation that something other than oneself is real. Love, and so art and morals, is the discovery of reality.
>
> (p. 215)

What a succinct, strange, beautiful formulation.

This feels like it's getting abstract, though. I suppose that's an occupational hazard of theoretical and philosophical psychologists. Let me therefore come back to what I, following in the footsteps of my philosophical support team, most want to say. I will be brief and to the point.

For all that I have called for a more open, inclusive, and pluralistic psychology, one that makes a suitable space for those regions of human experience that elude the grasp of science, as customarily conceived, I am really not sure whether moving in this direction suffices. Truthfully, I believe some aspects of contemporary psychology are positively destructive and give us a vision of inquiry, personhood, and *reality* that is inadequate and that undermines the kind of discipline psychology might—and ought to—be. At the same time, I don't want to conclude this book on a critical note and rehash all the reasons why I believe this to be so. Instead, I want to end on a note of hope—the hope that some of the words found in this book, and the spirit that animates them, which is not mine alone, will carry forth some of the energy, momentum, and care that are part of the project of promoting the psychological humanities.

It is time to move beyond critique, and it is time to move beyond acceding to the discipline's demands by trying to rework things or to create a more palatable version of what currently exists. It is time instead to do something new, something more adequate and faithful to human reality. I have no illusions about the speed with which this psychology might emerge. It is bound to take a good, long while. Patience is required. So too is humility—audacious humility, the kind that seeks to tear down the walls, gently, in the name of love.

References

Adichie, C. N. (2009). *The danger of a single story*. www.ted.com/talks/chimamanda_ngozi_adichie_the_danger_of_a_single_story
Bakhtin, M. (1986). *Speech genres and other late essays*. Univerity of Texas Press.
Barthes, R. (1989). *Roland Barthes*. The Noonday Press.
Bochner, A. P. (2001). Narrative's virtues. *Qualitative Inquiry*, *7*(2), 131–157.
Bochner, A. P., & Ellis, C. (2016). *Evocative autoethnography: Writing lives and telling stories*. Routledge.
Bonnefoy, Y. (1989). *The act and the place of poetry: Selected essays*. University of Chicago Press.
Bruner, J. (1987). Life as narrative. *Social Research*, *54*, 11–32.
Bruner, J. (1991). Self-making and world-making. *Journal of Aesthetic Education*, *25*, 67–78.
Buber, M. (1965). *Between man and man*. Macmillan.
Carr, D. L. (1986). *Time, narrative, and history*. Indiana University Press.
Charon, R. (2008). *Narrative medicine: Honoring the stories of illness*. Oxford University Press.
Csikszentmihalyi, M. (1990). *Flow: Toward a psychology of optimal experience*. Harper Collins.
Danto, A. C. (1985). *Narration and knowledge*. Columbia University Press.
Dawkins, R. (2008). *The God delusion*. Houghton Mifflin.
Ellis, C. (2009). *Revision: Autoethnographic reflections on life and work*. Left Coast Press.
Farley, W. (1996). *Eros for the other: Retaining truth in a pluralistic world*. Penn State University Press.
Flanagan, O. (1996). *Self expressions: Mind, morals, and the meaning of life*. Oxford University Press.
Flanagan, O. (2003). *The problem of the soul: Two visions of mind and how to reconcile them*. Basic.
Fowers, B. (2005). *Virtue ethics and psychology: Pursuing excellence in ordinary practices*. American Psychological Association.
Fowers, B., Richardson, F., & Slife, B. (2017). *Frailty, suffering, and vice: Flourishing in the face of human limitations*. American Psychological Association.
Frank, A. (1997). *The wounded storyteller: Body, illness, and ethics*. University of Chicago Press.
Freeman, M. (1984). History, narrative, and life-span developmental knowledge. *Human Development*, *27*, 1–19.

Freeman, M. (1985a). Paul Ricoeur on interpretation: The model of the text and the idea of development. *Human Development, 28*, 295–312.

Freeman, M. (1985b). Psychoanalytic narration and the problem of historical knowledge. *Psychoanalysis and Contemporary Thought, 8*, 133–182.

Freeman, M. (1989). After a fall. *Parenting, 112*.

Freeman, M. (1997). Death, narrative integrity, and the radical challenge of self-understanding: A reading of Tolstoy's *Death of Ivan Ilych. Ageing and Society, 17*, 373–398.

Freeman, M. (2000). Theory beyond theory. *Theory & Psychology, 10*, 71–77.

Freeman, M. (2002a). Charting the narrative unconscious: Cultural memory and the challenge of autobiography. *Narrative Inquiry, 12*, 193–211.

Freeman, M. (2002b). The presence of what is missing: Memory, poetry, and the ride home. In R. J. Pellegrini & T. R. Sarbin (Eds.), *Between fathers and sons: Critical incident narratives in the development of men's lives* (pp. 165–176). Haworth.

Freeman, M. (2002c). The burden of truth: Psychoanalytic *poiesis* and narrative understanding. In W. Patterson (Ed.), *Strategic narrative: New perspectives on the power of personal and cultural stories* (pp. 9–27). Lexington Books.

Freeman, M. (2003). Rethinking the fictive, reclaiming the real: Autobiography, narrative time, and the burden of truth. In G. Fireman, T. McVay, & O. Flanagan (Eds.), *Narrative and consciousness: Literature, psychology, and the brain* (pp. 115–128). Oxford University Press.

Freeman, M. (2007a). Wissenschaft und Narration (Science and story). *Journal für Psychologie, 15*(2). Retrieved October 25, 2007, from www.journal-fuer-psychologie.de/jfp-2-2007-5.html

Freeman, M. (2007b). Psychoanalysis, narrative psychology, and the meaning of "science". *Psychoanalytic Inquiry, 27*, 583–601.

Freeman, M. (2008a). Life without narrative? Autobiography, dementia, and the nature of the real. In G. O. Mazur (Ed.), *Thirty year commemoration to the life of A.R. Luria* (pp. 129–144). Semenko Foundation.

Freeman, M. (2008b). Beyond narrative: Dementia's tragic promise. In L.-C. Hydén & J. Brockmeier (Eds.), *Health, illness, and culture: Broken narratives* (pp. 169–184). Routledge.

Freeman, M. (2010). *Hindsight: The promise and peril of looking backward*. Oxford University Press.

Freeman, M. (2011). Toward poetic science. *Integrative Psychological and Behavioral Science, 45*, 389–396. http://doi.org/10.1007/s12124-011-9171-x

Freeman, M. (2012). Thinking and being Otherwise: Aesthetics, ethics, erotics. *Journal of Theoretical and Philosophical Psychology, 32*, 196–208.

Freeman, M. (2014a). *The priority of the Other: Thinking and living beyond the self.* Oxford University Press.

Freeman, M. (2014b). Qualitative inquiry and the self-realization of psychological science. *Qualitative Inquiry, 20*, 119–126.

Freeman, M. (2014d). Listening to the claims of experience: Psychology and the question of transcendence. *Pastoral Psychology, 63*, 323–337.

Freeman, M. (2015). Narrative psychology as science and as art. In J. Valsiner, G. Marsico, N. Chaudhary, T. Sato, & V. Dazzani (Eds.), *Psychology as a science of human being: The Yokohama manifesto* (pp. 349–364). Springer.

Freeman, M. (2018a). Discerning the history inscribed within: Significant sites of the narrative unconscious. In B. Wagoner (Ed.), *Handbook of culture and memory* (pp. 65–81). Oxford University Press.

Freeman, M. (2018b). Living in verse: Sites of the poetic imagination. In O. V. Lehmann, N. Chaudhary, A. C. Bastos, & E. Abbey (Eds.), *Poetry and imagined worlds* (pp. 139–154). Palgrave Macmillan.

Freeman, M. (2019a). Toward a poetics of the Other: New directions in post-scientific psychology. In T. Teo (Ed.), *Re-envisioning theoretical psychology: Diverging ideas and practices* (pp. 1–24). Palgrave Macmillan.

Freeman, M. (2019b). Heeding the face of the Other: A case study in relational ethics. *Human Arenas*, *2*, 416–432. https://doi.org/10.1007/s42087-019-00078-6

Freeman, M. (2020). Psychology as literature. Narrative knowing and the project of the psychological humanities. In J. Sugarman & J. Martin (Eds.), *A humanities approach to the psychology of personhood* (pp. 30–48). Routledge.

Freeman, M. (2021a). The mystery of identity: Fundamental questions, elusive answers. In M. Bamberg, C. Demuth, & M. Watzlawik (Eds.), *The Cambridge handbook of identity* (pp. 77–97). Cambridge University Press.

Freeman, M. (2021b). *Do I look at you with love? Reimagining the story of dementia*. Brill | Sense.

Freeman, M. (2021c). How does the world become ecstatic? Notes on the hermeneutics of transcendence. In R. Bishop (Ed.), *Hermeneutic dialogue and shaping the landscape of theoretical and philosophical psychology* (pp. 112–123). Routledge.

Freeman, M. (2022a). Narrative psychology and beyond: Returning the Other to the story of the self. In B. D. Slife, S. C. Yanchar, & F. C. Richardson (Eds.), *Routledge international handbook of theoretical and philosophical psychology: Critiques, problems, and alternatives to psychological ideas* (pp. 330–346). Routledge.

Freeman, M. (2022b). Poetry. In V. P. Glăveanu (Ed.), *The Palgrave encyclopedia of the possible*. Palgrave Macmillan. https://doi.org/10.1007/978-3-319-98390-5_226-1.

Freeman, M. (2023). The inevitability, and danger, of narrative. In H. Meretoja & M. Freeman (Eds.), *The use and abuse of storytelling: New directions in narrative hermeneutics* (pp. 15–35). Oxford University Press, Forthcoming.

Gadamer, H.-G. (1975). *Truth and method*. Crossroad.

Gadamer, H.-G. (1979). The problem of historical consciousness. In P. Rabinow & W. M. Sullivan (Eds.), *Interpretive social science: A reader* (pp. 82–140). University of California Press.

Gadamer, H.-G. (1986). *The relevance of the beautiful and other essays*. Cambridge University Press.

Gazzaniga, M. (1998). *The mind's past*. University of California Press.

Gergen, K. (2009). *Relational being: Beyond self and community*. Oxford University Press.

Goodman, D. (2012). *The demanded self: Levinasian ethics and identity in psychology*. Duquesne University Press.

Goodman, D., & Freeman, M. (2015). Introduction: Why the other? In D. Goodman & M. Freeman (Eds.), *Psychology and the other* (pp. 1–13). Oxford University Press.

Gusdorf, G. (1980). Conditions and limits of autobiography. In J. Olney (Ed.), *Autobiography: Essays theoretical and critical* (pp. 28–48). Princeton University Press (originally published 1956).

Harris, S. (2005). *The end of faith: Religion, terror, and the future of reason*. W.W. Norton.

Heaney, S. (1995). *The redress of poetry*. The Noonday Press.

Heidegger, M. (1971). *Poetry, language, thought*. Harper Colophon.

Heidegger, M. (1977). *The question concerning technology and other essays*. Harper Torchbooks.

Hydén, L. C., & Brockmeier, J. (Eds.). (2008). *Health, illness, and culture: Broken narratives*. Routledge.

James, W. (1950). *The principles of psychology: Volume one*. Dover (originally published 1890).
James, W. (1982). *The varieties of religious experience*. Penguin (originally published 1902).
Jung, C. G. (1933). *Modern man in search of a soul*. Harcourt Brace Jovanovich.
Kakutani, M. (2018). *The death of truth: Notes on falsehood in the age of Trump*. Penguin.
Kearney, R. (1998). *Poetics of imagining: Modernism to postmodernism*. Fordham University Press.
Kearney, R. (2001). *The God who may be: A hermeneutic of religion*. Indiana University Press.
Kearney, R. (2010). *Anatheism {returning to God after God}*. Columbia University Press.
Kerby, A. P. (1991). *Narrative and the self*. Indiana University Press.
Kirschner, S. R., & Martin, J. (Eds.). (2010). *The sociocultural turn: The contextual emergence of mind and self*. Columbia University Press.
Knausgaard, K. O. (2018). *Inadvertent*. Yale University Press.
Levinas, E. (1985). *Ethics and infinity*. Duquesne University Press.
Levinas, E. (1994). *Outside the subject*. Stanford University Press.
Levinas, E. (1996). Substitution. In A. T. Peperzak, S. Critchley, & R. Bernasconi (Eds.), *Emmanuel Levinas: Basic philosophical writings* (pp. 80–95). Indiana University Press.
Levinas, E. (1999). *Alterity and transcendence*. Columbia University Press.
Marcel, G. (1950). *The mystery of being, Vol. 1: Reflection and mystery*. Henry Regnery Co.
Marcuse, H. (1978). *The aesthetic dimension: Toward a critique of Marxist aesthetics*. Beacon.
Marion, J.-L. (2008). *The visible and the revealed*. Fordham University Press.
Maslow, A. (1970). *Religions, values, and peak experiences*. Penguin.
McAdams, D. P. (2006). The role of narrative in personality psychology today. *Narrative Inquiry*, *16*, 11–18.
McAdams, D. P., & McLean, K. C. (2013). Narrative identity. *Current Directions in Psychological Science*, *22*, 233–238.
McAdams, D. P., & Pals, J. L. (2006). A new big five: Fundamental principles for an integrative science of personality. *American Psychologist*, *61*, 204–217.
McIntyre, L. (2018). *Post-truth*. MIT Press.
McKibben, B. (2006). *The end of nature*. Random House.
Midgley, M. (2014). *Are you an illusion*? Acumen.
Murdoch, I. (1970). *The sovereignty of good*. Routledge.
Murdoch, I. (1993). *Metaphysics as a guide to morals*. Penguin.
Murdoch, I. (1999). *Existentialists and mystics: Writings on philosophy and literature*. Penguin.
Nussbaum, M. (1990). *Love's knowledge: Essays on philosophy and literature*. Oxford University Press.
Oliver, M. (2016). *Upstream*. Penguin.
Parini, J. (2008). *Why poetry matters*. Yale University Press.
Paz, O. (1967). *The bow and the lyre*. University of Texas Press.
Richardson, F. (2012). On psychology and virtue ethics. *Journal of Theoretical and Philosophical Psychology*, *32*, 24–34.
Ricoeur, P. (1970). *Freud: An essay on interpretation*. Yale University Press.
Ricoeur, P. (1973). The model of the text: Meaningful action considered as a text. *New Literary History*, *5*, 91–117.
Ricoeur, P. (1974). *The conflict of interpretations*. Northwestern University Press.

Ricoeur, P. (1981a). Narrative time. In W. J. T. Mitchell (Ed.), *On narrative* (pp. 165–186). University of Chicago Press.

Ricoeur, P. (1981b). The metaphorical process as imagination, cognition, and feeling. In M. Johnson (Ed.), *Philosophical perspectives on metaphor* (pp. 228–247). University of Minnesota Press.

Ricoeur, P. (1992). *Oneself as another*. University of Chicago Press.

Robinson, M. (2012). *When I was a child, I read books*. Picador.

Robinson, M. (2015). *The givenness of things*. Farrar, Straus and Giroux.

Robinson, M. (2018). *What are we doing here*? Farrar, Straus, and Giroux.

Scarry, E. (1999). *On beauty and being just*. Princeton University Press.

Schachtel, E. G. (1959). *Metamorphosis: On the conflict of human development and the problem of creativity*. Basic Books.

Singer, J. A. (2004). Narrative identity and meaning-making across the adult lifespan: An introduction. *Journal of Personality*, *72*, 437–459.

Slaney, K. (2020). The message in the medium: Knowing the psychological through art. In J. Sugarman & J. Martin (Eds.), *A humanities approach to the psychology of personhood* (pp. 8–29). Routledge.

Slife, B. (2004). Taking practices seriously: Toward a relational ontology. *Journal of Theoretical and Philosophical Psychology*, *24*, 179–195.

Solnit, R. (2014). *The faraway nearby*. Penguin.

Spencer, D. (2020). *Metagnosis: Revelatory narratives of health and identity*. Oxford University Press.

Steiner, G. (1989). *Real presences*. University of Chicago Press.

Steiner, G. (1997). *Errata: An examined life*. Yale University Press.

Stelter, B. (2018). *President Trump is willing the storytelling game, with help from his friends in the media*. https://money.cnn.com/2018/08/05/media/donald-trump-storytelling/index.html

Sugarman, J., & Martin, J. (2020a). Introduction. In *A humanities approach to the psychology of personhood* (pp. 1–7). Routledge.

Sugarman, J., & Martin, J. (Eds.). (2020b). *A humanities approach to the psychology of personhood*. Routledge.

Szymborska, W. (1996). *The poet and the world (Nobel Prize Lecture)*. www.nobelprize.org/prizes/literature/1996/szymborska/lecture/

Taylor, C. (1989). *Sources of the self: The making of modern identity*. Harvard University Press.

Teo, T. (2017). From psychological science to the psychological humanities: Building a general theory of subjectivity. *Review of General Psychology*, *21*, 281–291.

Teo, T. (2020). Theorizing in psychology: From the critique of a hyper-science to conceptualizing subjectivity. *Theory & Psychology*, *30*, 759–767.

Toulmin, S. (1990). *Cosmopolis: The hidden agenda of modernity*. University of Chicago Press.

Toulmin, S. (2001). *Return to reason*. Harvard University Press.

Weil, S. (1997). *Gravity and grace*. Routledge (originally published 1952).

Weintraub, K. (1975). Autobiography and historical consciousness. *Critical Inquiry*, *1*, 821–848.

Woods, J. (2015). *The nearest thing to life*. Brandeis University Press.

Index

For Product Safety Concerns and Information please contact our EU representative GPSR@taylorandfrancis.com Taylor & Francis Verlag GmbH, Kaufingerstraße 24, 80331 München, Germany

Printed and bound by CPI Group (UK) Ltd, Croydon, CR0 4YY
14/09/2026
02216243-0007